Is the Truth for Everybody?

RICKY CLEMONS

PUBLISHED BY FIDELI PUBLISHING, INC.

Copyright ©2024, Ricky Clemons
ALL RIGHTS RESERVED.

No part of this publication may be reproduced, stored in a retrieval system, or transmitted in any form or by any means—electronic, mechanical, photo-copy, recording, or any other—except for brief quotation in reviews, without the prior permission of the author or publisher.

ISBN: 978-8-8693-0151-2

Published by

Fideli Publishing, Inc.
119 W. Morgan St.
Martinsville, IN 46151
www.FideliPublishing.com

Table of Contents

Is the Truth for Everybody? 1
Tell the Truth 4
Our Purpose in Life 8
Jesus Sees Who You Can Become in Him 10
Don't Underestimate 12
Your 14
We Don't Have Time To 15
If Things Go Our Way All the Time 17
When the Lord Tells Us to do Something 19
Will Waste No Time 21
Benefits 23
Your Talents Will 24
Mr. Rush and Mr. Patient 26
Many People Love God's Creations 28
Control Over 30
There is Nothing New Under the Sun 32
No Special Privilege 34
Jesus Has Won the Victory Over Our 36
It Doesn't Take Much 38
Don't Worry 40
In My Mind and in My Heart 42
It's Truly You, Lord Jesus 44

Want to be Right	48
Like Heaven on Earth	50
Please Don't Shake Me Out of the Church	53
Down in the Depths of Your Love	55
Doesn't Take Pleasure In	56
We Will Not Get All the Answers	57
O Lord, You Foreknew	58
Can Seem to be Eternal	59
If We Make it to Heaven	61
Education	63
Lower Than	65
Who Can Know the Heart?	67
Are Better Than	69
The Truth Can Heal Anyone	71
O Lord, You Brought Me	73
Strayed Away from the Lord	75
Back Up into Our Faces	77
Many People Don't Talk About Jesus	79
God Will Not Change His Holy Word	83
It Doesn't Take Much at All	85
There is Nothing	87
If We Go	89
Many People Don't	92
Pure Works Unto the Lord	94

O Lord, Help Me 95

How We Grew Up 97

Just Because We 98

Living Our Life Unto the Lord 100

Only the Lord is Always Right 102

The Knowledge of God 104

In the Everlasting, Loving and Eternal Lord 105

To Anyone Who Loves the Lord 107

Words are Very Powerful 108

Sin Came into this World 110

Like a Heavy Downpour of Rain 112

I Have Some Rascal in Me 114

The Self-Checkout 115

Only Jesus Can Cleanse You from Your Sins 116

It's Always Easy for Jesus To 118

Completely Secured 120

We Will Have a Good Time 122

Forever and Ever is Not Long Enough 124

I Never Knew What it was Like 126

When I was a Wanderer 128

Sometimes, When We Believe 129

For a Display 130

Have Kept Silent 131

Our Lives Will be Like 132

The Earth's Ground 135
All Around the World... 137
Mentally Advanced and Emotionally Retarded 143
Christianity... 144
Carry Me Through 146
Many People Would Rather 147
The Lion's Den and Furnace Fire.. 149
The Highest Beauty 151
Before I Was Born 153
Questions.. 155
Ashamed 157
Will Not Reappear... 159
What are You Going to do with Me?...................................... 164
A Bad World... 165
Learning is Eternal 166
Are Like Trash.. 168
If Everything was Created by Chance.................................... 169
Youth Comes Around Once in Life 170
I Can't Say that I have Arrived 172
Light Cannot Agree with Darkness.. 173
Over the Rainbow 176

Is the Truth for Everybody?

God's holy word is the truth for everybody, whether we believe it or don't believe it.

God's holy word is the truth for everybody, whether we accept it or don't accept it.

God's holy word is the truth for everybody, whether we study it or don't study it.

God's holy word is the truth for everybody, whether we live by it or don't live by it.

God's holy word is the truth for everybody, whether we memorize it or don't memorize it.

God's holy word is the truth for everybody, whether we cherish it or don't cherish it.

God's holy word is the truth for everybody, whether we love it or don't love it.

God's holy word is the truth for everybody, whether we hear it or don't hear it.

God's holy word is the truth for everybody, whether we talk it or don't talk it.

God's holy word is the truth for everybody, whether we know it or don't know it.

God's holy word is the truth for everybody, whether we value it or don't value it.

God's holy word is the truth for everybody, whether we live in the country or live in the city.

God's holy word is the truth for everybody, whether we are good or bad.

God's holy word is the truth for everybody, whether we are rich, upper middle class, middle class, lower middle class or poor.

God's holy word is the truth for everybody, whether we are educated or not educated.

God's holy word is the truth for everybody, whether we are highly intelligent or averagely intelligent.

God's holy word is the truth for everybody, whether we are wise or foolish.

God's holy word is the truth for everybody, whether we are living free in society or locked up in prison.

God's holy word is the truth for everybody, whether we are well or sick.

God's holy word is the truth for everybody, whether we are successful or not successful.

God's holy word is the truth for everybody, whether we are inspired by it or not inspired by it.

God's holy word is the truth for everybody, whether we are joyful with it or not joyful with it.

God's holy word is the truth for everybody to get to know Jesus Christ, who will save us from our sins if we believe in Him so much more than anyone else and anything else in this world that has no heaven to put us in.

God's holy word is the truth for everybody, whether we spiritually eat it or don't spiritually eat it.

God's holy word is the truth for everybody, whether it makes us feel good or makes us feel bad.

God's holy word is the truth for everybody, whether it makes us feel guilty or doesn't make us feel guilty.

God's holy word is the truth for everybody, whether we are a Christian or an atheist.

God's holy word is the truth that God will not change for anyone under the sun and beyond the sun.

Tell the Truth

Thirty-four years ago, I was married to my first wife who is now deceased because of breast cancer that she had about twenty-two years ago.

Before I married her, I had no knowledge that she was manic depressive so I didn't seek any marriage counseling before I married her.

My first wife didn't like taking her medication for her manic depression and she would be violent toward me to the point that I got arrested and put in jail for defending myself because she was abusing me.

I was sentenced to four months in jail, and I had so much more peace there than I had living under the same roof with my first wife.

When I was in jail, I made friends with some of the inmates and we talked about the Lord and shared bible scriptures with one another.

I only had about three weeks left in jail when I witnessed two other inmates fighting on the indoor basketball court.

The correctional officer in the ward I was in wanted to know who started the fight.

The Lord put it in my heart to speak up and tell the truth about who started the fight.

A few days after I told the truth, I was transferred from minimum security to a maximum-security in jail.

In the maximum-security jail, I was placed in a cell with a murderer.

The whole cell block was filled with murderers and other violent criminals.

I know that the Lord was with me because no one in the cell block put me in harm's way or danger.

The Lord had truly given me the strength and the courage to not be afraid of those murderers and other violent criminals.

I was not afraid to talk about the Lord and His holy word when I was placed in the maximum-security jail cell.

I spoke plain and told the truth in the minimum-security jail about the fight that I witnessed.

Telling the truth caused me to be placed in the maximum-security facility.

The Lord put it in my heart to tell the truth about who started the fight on the basketball court.

Before I spoke up and told the truth, the inmate who did not start the fight was accused of starting it.

If telling the truth causes you to make enemies, then it is worth it because if God is for you then who can be against you for telling the truth?

If I had not obeyed the Lord, who put it in my heart to tell the truth, then there was no telling who else would have had the conscious to tell the truth.

It's sometimes difficult to tell the truth, whether you're locked up in jail or free in society every day.

The Lord foreknew that me telling the truth would encourage another jail inmate to tell the truth too.

Real, true bondage is telling lies, even if you and I are free as a bird flying up in the sky.

Not standing up for the truth, especially when it comes to God's holy word, is surely living a lie, whether you're locked up in jail or living free in society.

The devil meant it for my bad when I got locked up in jail for defending myself and trying to get away from my abusive first wife who refused to take her medication for her manic depression.

The Lord used me being locked up in jail for my good so I would stand up and tell the truth with boldness about who started the fight on the indoor basketball court.

I have no regrets about telling the truth, even though I was placed in the maximum-security jail where the Lord protected me from the worst kinds of criminals when I was there.

Telling the truth is freedom, even when you're locked up in jail where there is no freedom.

Telling the truth is freedom from the bondage of keeping silent about what you witness.

Keeping silent about the truth is like telling a lie, whether you and I are living free in society or we're locked up in jail.

True freedom is telling the truth.

The Lord loves the truth every day, and the truth sets us free from the devil's lies, even if you and I are locked up in jail.

Even though I was locked up in jail, I felt true freedom for telling the truth in that bondage environment where the Lord caused the worst kinds of criminals to make peace with me.

When I gave my life to the Lord, my mind was made up to tell the truth and live the truth unto the Lord who knew that my motives and intentions were true in my marriage to my first wife regardless of her manic-depressive disorder that was hard on her as well as being hard on me too.

I've learned that even in troubled times it is always good to tell the truth, even under hard circumstances in our lives.

The Lord hates a lying tongue and it will not go unpunished in the Lord's eyesight.

Telling the truth in love is splendor to the Lord, even if you and I are locked up in jail for doing something wrong that we did not plan to do.

When Jesus lived here on earth, He always told the truth even though the scribes and Pharisees did not believe Him and had caused Jesus to be crucified because they believed He was telling lies.

Jesus never kept silent about the truth that He foreknew would set people free from the devil's lies.

The devil didn't want anyone to believe that Jesus was the living truth sent from heaven by God to redeem all human beings back to God.

Jesus was never afraid to tell the truth to sinners being who we are.

Jesus Christ is the way, the truth and the life for you and me to tell the truth that has no wrongs for anyone not to tell the truth.

No matter what we do, the Lord will forgive us if we truly repent unto Him.

Our Purpose in Life

Our purpose in life is to love Jesus and keep his Commandments.

There is no other higher purpose than to love and obey Jesus Christ every day.

There is no other better purpose than to love Jesus and keep His Commandments.

Everybody's true purpose in life is to love Jesus and keep His Commandments.

Many people don't know their true purpose in life as they go through life being like a wanderer not knowing where they are going.

Knowing one's true purpose in life and living it will make the devil tremble in fear.

The devil wants us to believe that our purpose in life is to do our own will.

Loving Jesus and keeping His Commandments is our true purpose in this life and in the eternal life that we will receive if we are saved in Jesus Christ.

Our purpose in life is nothing less than loving Jesus and keeping His Commandments.

Many people believe that their purpose in life is to do whatever they want to do.

They believe that there is no God who is the origin of life who gave even all the animals and nature their purpose to exist.

Our purpose in life is to love Jesus and keep His Commandments for as long as we live.

There is no other true, glorious and perfect purpose that can out-do Jesus in blessing our lives for loving Him and keeping His Commandments.

Keeping Jesus' Commandments is everlasting beyond this world's temporary purpose that will come to an end for all who are lost in their sins for not loving Jesus and keeping His Commandments, which is every person's true purpose in life.

Jesus Sees Who You Can Become in Him

People will normally see your mistakes.

People will normally see your bad habits.

People will normally see your weaknesses.

People will normally see your flaws.

Jesus sees who you can become in Him if you confess and repent of your sins and live your life unto Him.

People will normally see your misfortunes.

People will normally see your insecurities.

People will normally see your fears.

People will normally see your problems.

People will normally see your faults.

People will normally see your worries.

Jesus sees who you can become in Him if you believe in Him.

People will normally see your wrongs.

People will normally see your selfishness.

People will normally see your pretenses.

People will normally see your enviousness.

People will normally see your jealousies.

People will normally see your brokenness.

Jesus sees who you can become in Him if you have a relationship with Him.

People will normally see your unfriendliness.

People will normally see your carelessness.

People will normally see your unconcern.

People will normally see your inadequacies.

People will normally see your inexperience.

People will normally see your lack of intelligence.

Jesus sees who you can become in Him If you deny yourself and pick up your cross and follow Him.

People will normally see your pride.

People will normally see your shyness.

People will normally see your impatience.

People will normally see your indifference.

Jesus sees who you can become in Him if you give all of your mind, heart and soul to Him.

People will normally see your outward appearance.

Jesus sees who you can become in Him even if your spiritual brothers and sisters in the church don't see how far Jesus can take you in your life for uplifting His holy name and living right unto Him every day.

Don't Underestimate

Don't underestimate what the Lord can do for anyone who loves and obeys Him.

Many people will underestimate people who are less talented than they are.

Many people will underestimate people who are less educated than they are.

Many people will underestimate people who are less fortunate than they are.

Many people will underestimate people who are less intelligent than they are.

Don't underestimate what the Lord can do for anyone who the Lord can allow to be great.

Don't underestimate who the Lord can allow to rise up above you and me.

Many people will underestimate those who are less healthy than they are.

Many people will underestimate those who are less financially stable than they are.

Many people will underestimate those who are less outgoing than they are.

Many people will underestimate those who are less prosperous than they are.

Don't underestimate what the Lord can do for anyone who is saved in Him.

Many people will underestimate those who are less skillful than they are.

Many people will underestimate those who are less alert than they are.

Many people will underestimate those who are less active than they are.

Many people will underestimate those who are less determined than they are.

Many people will underestimate those who are less attractive than they are.

Many people will underestimate those who are less talkative than they are.

Many people will underestimate those who are less wise than they are.

Many people will underestimate those who the Lord sees to be no less than you who the Lord will open the windows of heaven for and pour out His blessings upon for returning faithful tithes and offerings from even a small income that the Lord can greatly increase.

Don't underestimate yourself who can repent and live for the Lord Jesus Christ who the birds won't underestimate to feed them every day.

Your

Your mountains of problems may be high but not too high for Jesus to climb up to remove your problems.

Your oceans of pain may be deep but not too deep for Jesus to dive down to bring your pain to the surface of His healing power.

Your rivers of discouragement may be wide but not too wide for Jesus to cover with His encouragements in His holy word.

Your storms of troubles may be rough but not too rough for Jesus to smooth out in your life.

Your valley of fears may be low but not too low for Jesus to walk down in to comfort you.

Your shadow of death may be hopeless but not too hopeless for Jesus to give you hope to live and call on His holy name to be saved.

Your breath of life may be gloomy but not too gloomy for Jesus to vitalize your life for you to do His holy will.

Your genetics may be flawed but not too flawed for Jesus to cleanse you of your sins if you confess and repent of your sins unto Him.

Your choices may be unpredictable but not too unpredictable for Jesus to help you choose to love and obey Him.

God's holy word is the truth about the Lamb of God, without stains or blemishes, to save you from your sins.

We Don't Have Time To

We don't have time to keep the gospel of Jesus Christ to ourselves, because time is running out for souls to be saved in Jesus Christ.

We Christians must tell the world about Jesus coming back one day soon on the clouds of glory to take all to heaven who are saved in Him.

We don't have time to be putting things off when it comes to the salvation of people's souls.

We must tell the world about Jesus in sermons, songs, bible school lessons and in published books about Jesus, who gave up His life on the cross to save us all from our sins.

We don't have time to be unstable in our ways by saying one thing and doing another thing that is not like Jesus.

We don't have time to be tossed here and there like the wind blowing a house off of its foundation.

We need to be rooted and grounded in Jesus Christ, who doesn't have time to keep being patient with anyone who doesn't want to change from their wicked ways of living.

We Christians don't have time to not use our God-given spiritual gifts to edify the church that Jesus is the head of.

We have no time to listen to anyone's excuses for not trusting Him who cannot fail to bring anyone through their hardships.

We Christians don't have time to doubt what Jesus can do for us, even if we are on our death bed.

We can still believe that Jesus will give us eternal life which death can't take away from us.

We Christians especially don't have time to be wishy-washy in the presence of unbelievers who need to see Jesus living in us.

They need to know that we are stable in our ways because Jesus is our strong foundation that we can stand on in this quicksand and sinkhole world that will take anyone down to the bottomless pit of sin.

If Things Go Our Way All the Time

If things go our way all the time, then we would see no need to pray to the Lord.

If things go our way all the time, then we would see no need to wait on the Lord.

If things go our way all the time, then we would see no need to put our trust in the Lord.

If things go our way all the time, then we would see no need to worship the Lord.

If things go our way all the time, then we would see no need to go to church.

If things go our way all the time, then we would see no need to study the bible.

If things go our way all the time, then we would see no need to ask the Lord for anything.

If things go our way all the time, then we would see no need to believe in the Lord Jesus Christ.

If things go our way all the time, then we would see no need to deny oneself and pick up one's cross and follow Jesus Christ the Lord and Savior of the world.

If things go our way all the time, then we would see no need to obey the Lord.

If things go our way all the time, then we would see no need to be convicted of our sins.

If things go our way all the time, then we would see no need to be converted.

If things go our way all the time, then we would see no need to live our lives unto the Lord.

If things go our way all the time, then we would see no need to put our hope in the Lord.

If things go our way all the time, then we would see no need to give our heart to the Lord.

If things go our way all the time, then we would see no need to be thankful unto the Lord.

If things go our way all the time, then we would see no need to think on the Lord.

Because things don't go their way all the time, there are many people who won't pray to the Lord.

Because things don't go their way all the time, there are many people who won't put their trust in the Lord.

Because things don't go their way all the time, there are many people who won't obey the Lord.

Because things don't go their way all the time, there are many people who won't deny oneself and pick up one's cross and follow the Lord Jesus Christ.

We all were born in sin to be flawed with wanting everything to go our way.

The Lord knows that if He allows everything to go our way we would destroy ourselves and no one would be saved in Him.

There would be no such thing as being guilty for anyone if things go our way all the time.

Having things go our way all the time would cause everyone in this world to believe that they don't need to believe in Jesus Christ.

Only Jesus can handle everything, and only Jesus has everything going His way all the time when you and I can get a swelled head when even one thing goes our way.

When the Lord Tells Us to do Something

When the Lord tell us to do something, we must do it.

The Lord will not tell us to do something that He knows we can't do.

There are people who will tell us to do something that we can't do.

The Lord will tell us to do something that He knows we can do.

The Lord will never tell us to do something evil.

The Lord will never tell us to do something wrong.

The Lord will always tell us to do something right.

When the Lord tells us to do something, we must do it.

The Lord will always tell us to do something at the right time.

The Lord will never tell us to do something at the wrong time.

Whatever the Lord tells us to do, we must do it and not question Him.

Whatever the Lord tells us to do, we must do it and not put it off for another day.

Whatever the Lord tells us to do we must do it and not doubt Him.

Whatever the Lord tells us to do, we must do it with joy.

Whatever the Lord tells us to do, it will be for our good and for the good of others who especially love the Lord.

When the Lord tells us to do something, we must do it because it will be in line with His holy word.

When the Lord tells us to do something, we must do it because it will bless other people's lives.

When the Lord tells us to do something, we must do it so we will never regret it for not doing it.

When the Lord tells us to do something, we must do it even if it is confusing to us.

When the Lord tells us to do something, we must do it so it will give us a peace of mind.

When the Lord tells us to do something, we must do it so it will prosper us spiritually in a way that we need it most from day to day.

When the Lord tells us to do something, we must do it so it will glorify His holy name.

When the Lord tells us to do something, we must do it because it won't be more than what we can bear.

When the Lord tells us to do something, we must do it because it will strengthen our faith in the Lord.

When he Lord tells us to do something, we must do it to make the devil a defeated foe.

When the Lord tells us to do something, we must do it to cause the holy angels to rejoice in heaven.

When the Lord tells us to do something, we must do it so it will bless our lives.

When the lord tells us to do something, we must do it and know it won't embarrass us in any way.

When the Lord tells us to do something, we must do it and not change anything.

When the Lord tells us to do something, we must do it at the right time.

The Lord will not tell us to do something that will put us in an entanglement.

Will Waste No Time

The sun will waste no time to shine.

The moon will waste no time to glow.

The stars will waste no time to sparkle.

The birds will waste no time to fly.

The rivers will waste no time to flow.

The wind will waste no time to blow.

The grass will waste no time to grow.

The sky will waste no time to hover over us.

The clouds will waste no time to form.

The rain will waste no time to pour down on us.

The leaves will waste no time to fall on the ground.

Children will waste no time to play.

Trouble will waste no time to come our way.

Tornadoes will waste no time to destroy anything in their pathway.

Criminals will waste no time to do wrong.

The government will waste no time to conduct its policies.

Jesus will waste no time to save anyone from their sins if they confess and repent of their sins unto Him.

Jesus will waste no time to come back again on His own time when it will be too late for many people to be saved after rejecting Jesus.

Many people will waste no time to live in their sins but will waste a lot of time denying themselves and picking up their crosses to follow Jesus.

Many people will waste no time to do things of their own will but will waste a lot of time when it comes to doing things of the Lord's will.

The devil will waste no time to cause souls to be lost, but the Lord will waste no time to give His Holy Spirit to anyone who believes in Him.

God didn't waste any time sending His only begotten Son, Jesus Christ, to this sinful world to save us from our sins.

You and I will waste no time wanting to live if our life is in danger, but we can waste some time shunning away from the appearances of evil that are a danger to our spiritual life every day.

A baby will waste no time to cry out loud because of feeling some discomfort, but you and I can waste some time crying out loud unto the Lord with tears of joy about what the Lord brought us through for us to see this day.

We should waste no time to love and obey the Lord like it is our last day to live.

Benefits

There are no good benefits for being a slave for men.

There are good benefits for being a slave for Jesus Christ.

You won't have a peace of mind for being a slave for men.

You will have a peace of mind for being a slave for Jesus Christ.

You won't have any joy for being a slave for men.

You will have joy for being a slave for Jesus Christ.

You won't feel good about being a slave for men.

You will feel good about being a slave for Jesus Christ.

You won't have any freedom for being a slave for men.

You will have freedom for being a slave for Jesus Christ.

There are no good benefits for being a slave for men.

There are good benefits for being a slave for Jesus Christ.

You won't get any love for being a slave for men.

You will receive everlasting love for being a slave for Jesus Christ.

You won't be encouraged for being a slave for men.

You will be encouraged for being a slave for Jesus Christ.

You won't live a good life for being a slave for men.

You will receive an abundance of life for being a slave for Jesus Christ.

There are no good benefits for being a slave for men.

There are eternal good benefits for being a slave for Jesus Christ.

What good benefits would you and I get for being a slave for men?

If anything good comes out of being slave for men, the good is from the Lord Jesus Christ who owns everything.

Ungodly men have put many people into slavery to benefit them in obtaining what the Lord owns.

Your Talents Will

Your talents will lift you up more than they will lift anyone else up.

Your talents will bring out the best in you more than bringing out the best in anyone else.

Your talents will help you more than they will help anyone else.

Your talents will do you more good than they will do anyone else good.

Your talents will build you up more than they will build up anyone else.

Your talents will reassure you more than they will reassure anyone else.

Your talents will give you more joy than they will give joy to anyone else.

Your talents will give you more security than they will give to anyone else.

Your talents will give you more courage than they will give courage to anyone else.

Your talents will give you more peace the they will give peace to anyone else.

Your talents will give you more hope than they will give hope to anyone else.

Your talents are given to you from the Lord so you can glorify His holy name.

Your talents are from the Lord, who knows what talents you are to have.

Your talents are from the Lord, who gives you the talents you need to win souls in His name.

Your talents are from the Lord Jesus Christ, who gives you all the right talents to help you hold onto Him, even if all hell breaks loose in your life.

If you use your talents for the Lord, you won't become burdened.

You can choose to use your talents for the Lord or use your talents for your own selfish desires.

If you use your talents for the Lord, you will fulfill the true purpose in your life which belongs to the Lord.

Your talents can bless other people's lives, but they will bless your life the most, especially if you use your talents to glorify the Lord's holy name.

Mr. Rush and Mr. Patient

One day in the morning, Mr. Rush and Mr. Patient met each other for the first time.

They could see how different they were when Mr.

Rush said to Mr. Patient, "I've got to go right now."

Mr. Rush said to Mr. Patient, "I've got to do it right now."

Mr. Rush said to Mr. Patient, "I've got to say it right now."

Mr. Rush said to Mr. Patient, "I've got to leave right now."

Mr. Rush said to Mr. Patient, "I just can't wait on you."

Mr. Patient finally said to Mr. Rush, "You need to take your time when going where you want to go because rushing can cause you to fall off course."

Mr. Patient said to Mr. Rush, "You need to take your time when doing what you want to do because rushing can cause you to do something that you don't intend to do."

Mr. Patient said to Mr. Rush, "You need to take your time when saying what you want to say because rushing can cause you to say what you don't mean to say."

Mr. Patient said to Mr. Rush, "You need to take your time when leaving because rushing to leave can cause you to leave something behind."

Mr. Rush said to Mr. Patient, "I am not like you because I don't take my time; I want to do things right now.

Taking my time is moving too slow for me."

Mr. Patient said to Mr. Rush, "Suppose if Jesus had rushed to come to this world before the fullness of time."

Mr. Patient said to Mr. Rush, "If Jesus had rushed to come to this world to save sinners from being lost, then His mission would not have been accomplished.

"So many people would have been left out of God's saving grace, which is His patience for all sinners to eventually be saved in Jesus Christ.

"God was patient to send His Son, Jesus Christ, into this world while the devil was rushing to cause as many people as he could to be lost in their sins.

The devil is still rushing today to cause you and me to be lost in sin, while God is patient with us all today to confess and repent of our sins and believe in His Son, Jesus Christ, to be saved.

God's patience will run out one day and that is why the devil is in a big rush to cause as many souls as he can to be lost.

The Lord is patient to save as many souls as He can before it is too late and God will close His probation on this world when Jesus stands up and says that it is finished.

When that happens, those who are righteous will be righteous still and those who are filthy with sin will be filthy still."

Mr. Patient said to Mr. Rush, "Be patient and wait on the Lord and good things will come to you."

Many People Love God's Creations

Many people love God's creations but they don't love God.

Many people love the sunshine but they don't love God, who created the sun to shine.

Many people love the full white moonlight but they don't love God, who created the moon that reflects its light onto us.

Many people love the stars that sparkle in the night sky but they don't love God, who created the stars that sparkle in the night sky.

Many people love the mountains but they don't love God, who created the mountains.

Many people love the oceans but they don't love God, who created the oceans.

Many people love the flowers but they don't love God, who created the flowers.

Many people love God's creations, but they don't love God.

Many people love the sky but they don't love God, who created the sky.

Many people love the rain but they don't love God, who created the rain.

Many people love the snow but they don't love God, who created the snow.

Many people love God's creations but they don't love God.

Many people love the trees but they don't love God, who created the trees.

Many people love the grass but they don't love God, who created the grass.

Many people love the dry land but they don't love God, who created the dry land.

Many people love animals but they don't love God who created the animals.

Many people love the birds but they don't love God who created the birds.

Many people love this world but they don't love God who created this world.

Many people love God's creations but they don't love God and don't worship God.

Control Over

We do have control over the choices we make.

We have no control over an accident.

We have no control over the insects.

We have no control over the weather.

We do have control over the choices we make.

We have no control over the wind.

We have no control over the sea.

We have no control over the river.

We do have control over the choices we make.

We have no control over the seasons.

We have no control over the rain.

We have no control over the heat.

We do have control over the choices that we make.

We have no control over the cold chill.

We have no control over the past.

We have no control over the present.

We have no control over the future.

We do have control over the choices we make.

We have no control over the sunshine.

We have no control over the full white moonlight.

We have no control over the stars.

We have no control over a hurricane.

We do have control over the choices we make.

We have no control over a tornado.

We have no control over a flood.

We have no control over a natural disaster.

We have no control over a mystery.

We have no control over a phenomenon.

We do have control over the choices we make.

We have no control over a dream.

We have no control over an earthquake.

We have no control over death.

We have no control over the day.

We have no control over the night.

We do have control over the choices we make every day.

No one can say that they can't control their choices.

If the Lord knew that we couldn't control choices we make, then the Lord would not have given us a free will to choose.

We can control what we say and do.

A wicked man has control over his choices and can choose to do something evil.

We all have control over our choice to do good or evil.

The Lord has given us all a free will that allows us to have control over our choices, and the devil can't take that choice away from us.

We can't blame God or the devil for the bad choices we make.

The devil can only tempt us to make the wrong choice; he can't control the choices we make every day because God has given us a free will to choose and God will not control that choice.

We do have control over the choices we make, and we can trust that God will be a fair judge of our free will choices we make in our words and actions every day.

There is Nothing New Under the Sun

Some other people have probably said what you say.

Some other people have probably thought what you think.

Some other people have probably felt what you feel.

There is nothing new under the sun.

Some other people have probably understood what you understand.

Some other people have probably done what you do.

Some other people have probably seen what you see.

Some other people have probably heard what you hear.

There is nothing new under the sun.

Some other people have probably been where you go.

Some other people have probably dreamed what you dream.

Some other people have probably hoped for what you hope for.

Some other people probably ate what you eat.

Some other people have probably drunk what you drink.

There is nothing new under the sun.

Some other people have probably experienced that you experience.

Some other people have probably suffered what you suffer.

Some other people have probably accomplished what you want to accomplish.

Some other people have probably chosen what you choose.

There is nothing new under the sun.

The sun goes back to the beginning of time here on earth where there were many people who lived before you and me who did some things that we do today under the sun.

God created only one human race of people under the sun, the place where we all have something in common, whether that be saying or doing things that are right or wrong.

Under the sun we will all reap what we sow.

Under the sun we all can be saved in Jesus Christ, if we believe in Him and confess and repent of our sins and live for Jesus under the sun.

No Special Privilege

No person has special privilege over anyone else when it comes to You, my Lord and Savior Jesus Christ.

You, my Lord, love everyone equally every day.

O Lord, You don't love the president of the United States more than You love the trash man.

You, my Lord, don't love the rich man more than You love the poor man.

No one has special privilege over anyone else when it comes to You, my Lord and Savior Jesus Christ.

You, my Lord, don't love a healthy man more than You love a sick man.

You, my Lord, don't love an educated man more than You love an uneducated man.

O Lord, you don't love a wise man more than You love a foolish man.

No one has special privilege over anyone else when it comes to You, my Lord and Savior Jesus Christ.

You, O Lord, don't love the preacher more than You love the usher.

You, O Lord, don't love a saint more than You love a sinner.

No one has special privilege when it comes to You, My Lord and Savior Jesus Christ.

You, O Lord, don't love the white man more than You love the black man.

O Lord, You will never give any special privilege to anyone because You love everyone the same way every day.

The problem is that many people will give special privilege to certain people, even in the church that You, O Lord, are the head of.

No one has special privilege over anyone else when it comes to You, my Lord and Savior Jesus Christ.

You gave up Your life to save all men from their sins with no special privileges given to anyone to be more accepted by God to enter heaven.

Jesus Has Won the Victory Over Our

Jesus has won the victory over our bad habits.

Jesus has won the victory over our fears.

Jesus has won the victory over our weaknesses.

Jesus has won the victory over our disappointments.

Jesus has won the victory over our doubts.

Jesus has won the victory over our discouragements.

Jesus has won the victory over our ignorance.

Jesus has won the victory over our mistakes.

Jesus has won the victory over our failures.

Jesus has won the victory over our misfortunes.

Jesus has won the victory over our sorrows.

Jesus has won the victory over our brokenness.

Jesus has won the victory over our insecurities.

Jesus has won the victory over our bad days.

Jesus has won the victory over our depression.

Jesus has won the victory over our stress.

Jesus has won the victory over our frustrations.

Jesus has won the victory over our bondage.

Jesus has won the victory over our emptiness.

Jesus has won the victory over our waywardness.

Jesus has won the victory over our unbelief.

Jesus has won the victory over our lostness.

Jesus has won the victory over our sins.

Jesus has won the victory over everything that we go through in life.

Jesus has won the victory over our minds.

Jesus has won the victory over our hearts.

Jesus has won the victory over our lives for us to live doing His holy will that the devil can't ever break into pieces.

If Jesus had not been victorious on the cross for our sins and had not risen from the grave defeating death, then we all would be better off to have never been born than to live doomed to die in hell.

What good would our choices of free will be if Jesus had not been victorious over our sins allowing us to confess and repent and be saved in Him?

If Jesus had not been victorious over our sins, then we would all be doomed to be lost and for our free will to be condemned by God no matter what good choices we make because they would be so worthless if Jesus had not been victorious to win us the destiny to heaven that we don't deserve.

It Doesn't Take Much

It doesn't take much to get in an accident.

It doesn't take much to eat what we shouldn't eat.

It doesn't take much to drink what we shouldn't drink.

It doesn't take much to get into trouble.

It doesn't take much to be in the wrong place at the wrong time.

It doesn't take much to say something wrong.

It doesn't take much to do something wrong.

It doesn't take much to think wrong.

It doesn't take much to go into debt.

It doesn't take much to overspend.

It doesn't take much to get sick.

It doesn't take much to make a bad choice.

It doesn't take much to get killed.

It doesn't take much to have a bad habit.

It doesn't take much to give up.

It doesn't take much to fill yourself full of pride.

It doesn't take much to be selfish.

It doesn't take much for Jesus to show mercy on us.

It doesn't take much for Jesus to give us a second chance.

It doesn't take much for Jesus to save us from our sins.

It doesn't take much for Jesus to cleanse us from our sins.

It doesn't take much for Jesus to forgive us for our sins.

It doesn't take much for Jesus to love us.

It doesn't take much for Jesus to heal us.

It doesn't take much for Jesus to protect us.

It doesn't take much for Jesus to rescue us.

It doesn't take much for Jesus to supply all of our needs.

It doesn't take much for Jesus to bless us.

It doesn't take much for Jesus to spare our lives from death.

It doesn't take much for Jesus to add more years to our lives.

It doesn't take much for Jesus to give us His Holy Spirit.

It doesn't take much for Jesus to understand us.

It doesn't take much for Jesus to be for us.

It doesn't take much for Jesus to encourage us.

It doesn't take much for Jesus to give us joy.

It doesn't take much for Jesus to live in us.

It doesn't take much for Jesus to give us the victory.

It doesn't take much for Jesus to be our best friend.

It doesn't take much for Jesus to give us a peace of mind.

It doesn't take much for Jesus to give us courage.

It doesn't take much for Jesus to give us wisdom.

It doesn't take much for Jesus to answer our prayers.

It doesn't take much for Jesus to give us justice.

It doesn't take much for Jesus to give us His righteousness.

It doesn't take much for Jesus to accept us when we come to Him, because He won't reject us for confessing and repenting of our sins unto Him.

Don't Worry

Do what you need to do and don't worry.

Say what you need to say and don't worry.

Eat what you need to eat and don't worry.

Drink what you need to drink and don't worry.

Go where you need to go and don't worry.

Don't worry about things you have no control over.

Don't worry about what you should have said.

Don't worry about what you didn't say.

Don't worry about what you should have done.

Don't worry about what you didn't do.

Don't worry about what you did wrong.

Don't worry about what you don't know.

Don't worry about what you don't remember.

Don't worry about how you feel.

Don't worry about what you have to do.

Don't worry about tomorrow.

Don't worry about what you didn't do today.

Don't worry about what you can't do.

Don't worry about the mistake that you made.

Don't worry about how you will make it through the day.

Don't worry about being disappointed.

Don't worry about being rejected.

Don't worry about being disrespected.

Don't worry about what you lost.

Don't worry about what you messed up.

Don't worry about what you did in the past.

Don't worry about what you can't change.

Don't worry about making a mistake.

Don't worry about what you don't have.

Don't worry about what you overlooked.

Don't worry about what you have to give up.

Don't worry about who doesn't love you.

Don't worry about who doesn't support you.

Don't worry about what you didn't achieve.

Don't worry about what you fear.

Jesus foreknew that He would have to be beaten and shed His blood on the cross and die on the cross to save us from our sins.

Jesus didn't worry about what He had to do because He stayed in prayer unto His heavenly Father who gave Him the strength that He needed to accomplish His mission here on earth.

We don't have to worry about anything because Jesus is victorious over whatever problem or bad situation that comes our way on any day.

We can put all of our trust in Jesus to ease our minds from worries.

Worrying won't solve our problems because Jesus solves our problems.

Worrying won't make things better because Jesus can make it better.

Is worrying our master or is Jesus our master?

Who will we serve through our troubled times?

In My Mind and in My Heart

I believe in my mind that You, Lord Jesus, are the Son of God, and I need to love you, O Lord, in my heart.

I believe in my mind that You, Lord Jesus, are the way, the truth and the life, but in my heart, I need to trust You.

I believe in my mind that You, Lord Jesus, do answer my prayers, but in my heart, I need to wait on You to answer my prayers.

I believe in my mind that You, Lord Jesus, cannot fail me, but in my heart, I need to claim my victory in You.

I believe in my mind that You, Lord Jesus, will forgive me of my sins, but in my heart, I need to confess and repent of my sins unto You.

I believe in my mind that You, Lord Jesus, can cleanse me from my sins and save me from my sins, but in my heart, I need to not hold onto my sins.

I believe in my mind that You, Lord Jesus, will not condemn my heart but in my heart, I need to not condemn myself.

I believe in my mind that You, Lord Jesus, brought me this far in my life, but in my heart, I need to let go of all the wrongs that I have done.

I believe in my mind that You, Lord Jesus, will never change on me, but in my heart, I need to not change on You.

I believe in my mind that You, Lord Jesus, are the word of God, but in my heart, I need to live my life unto You who speaks the holy word.

I believe in my mind that You, Lord Jesus, are coming back again, but in my heart, I need to pray and watch and live my life like You could come back again on any day.

What I believe in my mind and in my heart can be different, but You, Lord Jesus, truly know my mind and my heart to bring them on one accord in You.

My mind and my heart must come together to please You, my Lord and Savior Jesus Christ, who has given me a mind that believes in You and a heart that loves You.

My Lord Jesus Christ, You gave me a mind to choose right from wrong and You gave me a heart to live right from wrong.

If I don't choose you, Lord Jesus, in my mind every day, then I won't live for You in my heart day after day.

I can't separate my mind and my heart from You, my Lord Jesus, and believe that my life is in harmony with You.

O, my Lord and Savior Jesus Christ, the demons believe that You are the Son of God who kicked them out of heaven because they stopped loving You.

The mind can be very powerful.

It can cause you and me to believe that we can walk on the water just like Jesus walked on water.

Peter walked on water until he began to look at the rugged waves fearfully.

What can a mind really accomplish without the heart?

What can the heart really accomplish without the mind?

The mind and heart must go hand in hand with the Lord, so we can uplift and glorify His holy name inside the church and outside the church.

It's Truly You, Lord Jesus

It's truly You, Lord Jesus, who brings people out of their hardships, yet many people don't give You the glory and praise.

It's truly You, Lord Jesus, who spares people's lives from death, yet many people don't give You the glory and praise.

It's truly You, Lord Jesus, who allows people to prosper, yet many people don't give You the glory and praise.

It's truly You, Lord Jesus, who allows people to become rich, yet many people don't give you the glory and praise.

It's truly You, Lord Jesus, who allows people to get fame, yet many people don't give You the glory and praise.

It's truly You, Lord Jesus, who allows people to heal, yet many people don't give You the glory and praise.

It's truly You, Lord Jesus, who gives talents to people, yet many people don't give You the glory and praise.

It's truly You, Lord Jesus, who gives people a second chance, yet many people don't give You the glory and praise.

Many people will give the glory and praise to luck.

Many people will give the glory and praise to men and women.

Many people will give the glory and praise to their children or even to their pets.

It's truly You, Lord Jesus, who gives everybody life, yet many people don't give You the glory and praise.

All the glory and praise belong to You, Lord Jesus, every day.

It's truly You, Lord Jesus, who created all things, yet many people don't give You the glory and praise.

It's truly You, Lord Jesus, who gives freedom, yet many people don't give You the glory and praise.

It's truly You, Lord Jesus, who gives justice, yet many people don't give You the glory and praise.

It's truly You, Lord Jesus, who gives equality, yet many people don't give You the glory and praise.

It's truly You, Lord Jesus, who gives peace, yet many people don't give You the glory and praise.

It's truly You, Lord Jesus, who gives all good things, yet many people don't give You the glory and praise.

It's truly You, Lord Jesus, who gives skills, yet many people don't give You the glory and praise.

It's truly You, Lord Jesus, who gives genius, yet many people don't give You the glory and praise.

It's truly You, Lord Jesus, who gives intelligence, yet many people don't give You the glory and praise.

It's truly You, Lord Jesus, who gives wisdom, yet many people don't give You the glory and praise.

It's truly You, Lord Jesus, who gives knowledge, yet many people don't give You the glory and praise.

It's truly You, Lord Jesus, who gives common sense, yet many people don't give You the glory and praise.

It's truly You, Lord Jesus, who gives education yet, many people don't give You the glory and praise.

It's truly You, Lord Jesus, who gives all the truth, yet many people don't give You the glory and praise.

It's truly You, Lord Jesus, who gives good laws, yet many people don't give You the glory and praise.

It's truly You, Lord Jesus, who gives good healthy food, yet many people don't give You the glory and praise.

It's truly You, Lord Jesus, who gives clean water to drink, yet many people don't give You the glory and praise.

It's truly You, Lord Jesus, who gives love, yet many people don't give You the glory and praise.

It's truly You, Lord Jesus, who gives good mental health, yet many people don't give You the glory and praise.

It's truly You, Lord Jesus, who gives good physical health, yet many people don't give You the glory and praise.

It's truly You, Lord Jesus, who gives good weather, yet many people don't give You the glory and praise.

It's truly You, Lord Jesus, who deserves all the glory and praise because You are good all the time.

You sustain life and you keep life going on beyond the dead.

It's truly You, Lord Jesus, who gives a way to escape the devil's worst kinds of temptations so he is not overbearing, yet many church folks don't give You the glory and praise.

It's truly You, Lord Jesus, who gives warnings, yet many young people don't give You the glory and praise.

These young people will commit sins unto their death.

It's truly You, Lord Jesus, who gives mercy and grace, yet many people don't give You the glory and praise.

These people will live their lives under their own will and will keep breaking Your golden rules until they are on their death beds.

They will blame You, Lord Jesus, for their foolish choices that You had nothing to do with.

It's truly You, Lord Jesus, who gives good hygiene, yet many people don't give You the glory and praise.

It's truly You, Lord Jesus, who gives protection, yet many people don't give You the glory and praise.

It's truly You, Lord Jesus, who gives good judgement, yet many people don't give You the glory and praise.

It's truly You, Lord Jesus, who gives boldness, yet many people don't give You the glory and praise.

It's truly You, Lord Jesus, who gives victory, yet many people don't give You the glory and praise.

It's truly You, Lord Jesus, who gives encouragement, yet many people don't give You the glory and praise.

It's truly You, Lord Jesus, who gives joy, yet many people don't give You the glory and praise.

It's truly You, Lord Jesus, who gives temperance, yet many people don't give You the glory and praise.

It's truly You, Lord Jesus, who gives goodness, yet many people don't give You the glory and praise.

It's truly You, Lord Jesus, who gives perfection, yet many people don't give You the glory and praise.

It's truly You, Lord Jesus, who gives corrections, yet many people don't give You the glory and praise.

It's truly You, Lord Jesus, who gives discipline, yet many people don't give You the glory and praise.

It's truly You, Lord Jesus, who gives blessings, yet many people don't give You the glory and praise.

No one can out-give You, Lord Jesus, on any day.

No one can out-give You, Lord Jesus, no matter how rich they are.

No one can out-give You, Lord Jesus, no matter how good they are.

It's truly You, Lord Jesus, who gives the heavens and other worlds eternal life and they give You all the glory and praise.

It's truly You, Lord Jesus, who gives existence its presence in the heavens and other worlds and in billions of galaxies that give You all the glory and praise beyond this sinful world where many people don't give You, Lord Jesus, the glory and praise for anything that You give to them.

Want to be Right

We all want to be right about what we think.

We all want to be right about what we do.

A little child wants to be right about what he or she thinks, says and does.

Even a criminal wants to be right about what he or she thinks, says, and does.

Nobody likes to be wrong, even if they are wrong.

Many people are so focused on wanting to be right that they don't care about anyone else being right in what he or she thinks, says and does.

Many people want to be right about what they feel and refuse to give a second thought to how someone else feels.

Wanting to be right all the time can surely be selfish and nobody likes to be wrong because that can be selfish too.

Everybody has a habit of wanting to be right in everyone's eyes, even when it comes to talking about the bible scriptures that many people can interpret in different ways.

Nobody will think correctly all the time.

Nobody will say the right words all the time.

Nobody will do the right thing all the time.

We were all born in sin to fall short by thinking wrong, saying something wrong and doing something wrong in the spur of the moment.

We all fall short of the glory of God because of being born in the sin that Adam and not Eve brought upon all the world to be so wrong to God.

We all want to be right about what we think and say and do because we don't like to be wrong.

Many people will be taken the wrong way for being right, especially when it comes to God's holy word.

God's holy word is right all the time, but there are people who will interpret it in the wrong way and they will believe that they are right.

Only Jesus was right all the time when He lived on Earth, especially when the scribes and Pharisees believed that they were right all the time and rejected Jesus because they didn't care about being wrong in His eyes.

Like Heaven on Earth

There are people who are like heaven on earth because they are so good.

There are people who are like heaven on earth because they are so kind.

There are people who are like heaven on earth because they are so gentle.

There are people who are like heaven on earth because they are so loving.

There are people who are like heaven on earth because they are so supportive.

There are people who are like heaven on earth because they are so understanding.

There are people who are like heaven on earth because they are so forgiving.

There are people who are like heaven on earth because they are so encouraging.

There are people who are like heaven on earth because they are so likeable.

There are people who are like heaven on earth because they are so joyful.

There are people who are like heaven on earth because they are so fair.

There are people who are like heaven on earth because they are so giving.

There are people who are like heaven on earth because they are so honest.

There are people who are like heaven on earth because they are so trustworthy.

There are people who are like heaven on earth because they are so friendly.

There are people who are like heaven on earth because they are so caring.

There are people who are like heaven on earth because they are so positive.

There are people who are like heaven on earth because they are so helpful.

There are people who are like heaven on earth because they are so wonderful.

There are people who are like heaven on earth because they are so peaceful.

There are people who are like heaven on earth because they are so respectful.

There are people who are like heaven on earth because they are so polite.

There are people who are like heaven on earth because they are so compassionate.

There are people who are like heaven on earth because they are so inspiring.

There are people who are like heaven on earth because they are so faithful.

There are people who are like heaven on earth because they are so patient.

There are people who are like heaven on earth because they are so tolerate.

There are people who are like heaven on earth because they are so obedient.

There are people who are like heaven on earth because they are so holy.

There are people who are like heaven on earth because they are so temperate.

There are people who are like heaven on earth because they are so selfless.

There are people who are like heaven on earth because they are so humble.

There are people who are like heaven on earth because they are so much like Jesus Christ, who is coming back again one day soon to take us to the real true heaven if we are saved in Him.

No one can be like heaven more than Jesus Christ, who was the real true heaven on earth when He lived on earth without sin.

Please Don't Shake Me Out of the Church

O Lord, please don't shake me out of the church because I want to believe in You every day.

O Lord, please don't shake me out of the church because I want to put my hope in You every day.

O Lord, please don't shake me out of the church because I want to worship You every day.

O Lord, please don't shake me out of the church because I want to put my trust in You every day.

O Lord, please don't shake me out of the church because I want to deny myself and pick up my cross and follow You every day.

O Lord, please don't shake me out of the church because I want to love You and keep your Commandments every day.

O Lord, please don't shake me out of the church because I want to have a relationship with You every day.

O Lord, please don't shake me out of the church because I want to keep my eyes on You every day.

O Lord, please don't shake me out of the church because I want to hold onto You every day.

O Lord, please don't shake me out of the church because I want to give You all of my heart every day.

O Lord, please don't shake me out of the church because I want to confess and repent of my sins unto You every day.

O Lord, please don't shake me out of the church because I want to be saved in You every day.

O Lord, please don't shake me out of the church because I want to live my life unto You every day.

O Lord, please don't shake me out of the church because I want to glorify and praise Your holy name every day.

O Lord, please don't shake me out of the church because I want to be a witness of You every day.

O Lord, please don't shake me out of the church because I want to be like You every day.

O Lord, please don't shake me out of the church because I want to know Your holy word every day.

O Lord, please don't shake me out of the church because I want to live by Your holy word every day.

O Lord, please don't shake me out of the church because I want to be watchful every day to see You coming back again on the clouds of glory one day.

O Lord, please don't shake me out of the church because I want to keep myself humble unto You every day.

O Lord, please don't shake me out of the church because I want to show reverence to You every day.

O Lord, please don't shake me out of the church because I want to be filled with Your holy spirit every day.

Down in the Depths of Your Love

O Lord, You have taken my broken heart down in the depths of Your love.

O Lord, You have taken my wayward mind down in the depths of Your love.

O Lord, You have taken my insecure thoughts down in the depths of Your love.

O Lord, You have taken my hopeless words down in the depths of Your love.

O Lord, You have taken my troubled life down in the depths of Your love.

O Lord, You have taken my ill feelings down in the depths of Your love.

O Lord, You have taken my mistakes down in the depths of Your love.

O Lord, You have taken my bad choices down in the depths of Your love.

O Lord, You have taken my selfish ways down in the depths of Your love.

O Lord, You have taken my ignorance down in the depths of Your love.

O Lord, Your love is deeper than my mind.

O Lord, Your love is deeper than my life.

O Lord, Your love is deeper than my destiny that can't surpass Your love for me because out of Your love, You gave me a free will to choose my destiny.

O Lord, you have taken my past and will take my present and future down in the depths of Your love for me to have no excuse to tell You on that great judgement day why I couldn't love You.

Doesn't Take Pleasure In

The Lord doesn't take pleasure in punishing anyone because the Lord God loves everybody enough to be saved in His Son, Jesus Christ.

Parents who love their children don't take pleasure in punishing their children for doing something that they have told them not to do.

Pet owners who love their pets don't take pleasure in punishing their spoiled pets that can do something to get on our nerves.

The Lord doesn't take pleasure in chastising you and me who He loves with an everlasting love.

Many people will take pleasure in living in sin when the Lord doesn't take pleasure in destroying anyone in their sins.

The Lord took no pleasure in casting Lucifer and his fallen angels out of heaven.

The Lord took no pleasure in putting Adam and Eve out of the Garden of Eden.

The Lord took no pleasure in destroying everybody in the flood, except eight people and some animals.

The Lord took no pleasure in destroying Sodom and Gomorrah in fire and brimstone.

The Lord will take no pleasure in destroying the devil and his fallen angels and his human agents in hell's fire and brimstone after the thousand years is up for all the holy saints to leave heaven and come back to this world in the new Jerusalem holy city.

The Lord's divine nature is nothing but everlasting love and He takes no pleasure in destroying what He created that is His strange act out of His eternal loving character.

We Will Not Get All the Answers

We will not get all the answers to our questions in this lifetime here on earth.

Many people have some hard questions that will not get answered because no one in this world has the answer to every question.

Only Jesus could answer everyone's questions when He lived here on earth without sin.

There are a lot of bible scholars who can answer several questions regarding the bible, but they can't answer every question.

Many people will have intelligent questions that can't be answered by even the greatest bible scholars, because even they fall short of God's glory.

We will not get the answers to all our questions until we arrive in heaven where Jesus will answer our every question.

All the questions that we don't get answered during our lifetime here on earth will be answered when Jesus comes back again to take us to heaven if we are saved in Him.

If anyone in this world had all the right answers to everyone's questions, then people would wonder if he or she was God.

Many people would bow down and worship that man or woman if they could answer all of their questions correctly, but only Jesus can do that and will do that when He comes back again to take all of His children to heaven and answer all of our questions correctly.

We will not get all the answers to our questions in this lifetime here on earth because we all were born in sin to not be able to handle all of Jesus' answers to our questions.

All of Jesus' answers are perfect and righteous beyond our smartest questions that will fall short of the glory of God.

O Lord, You Foreknew

O Lord, You foreknew that sinful men and sinful women would try to reach other worlds with their astronomy technology.

O Lord, You created this world, and You foreknew that sinful men and sinful women would create spacecrafts to try to go to other planets.

O Lord, You put those other perfect worlds so far away from this world so there would be no contact.

O Lord, You will not allow sinful men and sinful women to reach to those other worlds that are too far away for mortal men and women to reach.

They would age old and die before they reached those other worlds.

O Lord, You foreknew that You had to distance those other worlds from our sinful world because sinful men and sinful women would try to travel to other perfect worlds that will not allow sin to enter.

O Lord, You put a limit on sin for it to only be in this world, even though it was never in Your will for sin to exist in this once-perfect world.

O Lord, You will not let sin reach other perfect worlds You created for Your pleasure like you created this world for your pleasure until Adam and Eve sinned against You.

O Lord, You foreknew that astronomers would want to try to travel to the other worlds that You placed so far away from this sinful world.

You, Lord Jesus, knew that sinful men and women would want to live in other perfect worlds with their sins that heaven will not accept.

Can Seem to be Eternal

A bad storm can seem to be eternal until the storm is over.

A sickness can seem to be eternal until you get well.

A war can seem to be eternal until the war is over.

Being overweight can seem to be eternal until you lose some weight.

A heartache can seem to be eternal until you find love again.

Grief can seem to be eternal until time heals your broken spirit.

Trouble can seem to be eternal until you get out of trouble.

Gossip can seem to be eternal until you don't listen to it.

Injustice can seem to be eternal until you get justice.

Anger can seem to be eternal until you calm down.

The rain can seem to be eternal until it stops raining.

A hurricane can seem to be eternal until it is over.

A tornado can seem to be eternal until it is over.

An earthquake can seem to be eternal until it is over.

The day can seem to be eternal until the night comes in.

The night can seem to be eternal until the morning light comes in.

A broken bone can seem to be eternal until it heals.

A divorce can seem to be eternal until you get married again.

A mistake can seem to be eternal until you are forgiven.

A crime can seem to be eternal until you stop committing the crime.

Being in danger can seem to be eternal until you are out of danger.

Guilt can seem to be eternal until you confess and repent of your sins unto the Lord Jesus Christ who will save you from being lost in your sins for believing in Him, who is eternal life beyond anything that can seem to be eternal to you and me.

What can seem to be eternal to you and me is only a brief moment to Jesus, who can send an angel from heaven to earth quicker than a blink of an eye.

Death can seem to be eternal until Jesus Christ comes back again and raises the righteous dead to live with Him in heaven as if death never existed.

If We Make it to Heaven

If we make it to heaven, Jesus will give us an eternal mind.

If we make it to heaven, Jesus will give us an eternal body.

If we make it to heaven, Jesus will give us his eternal technology.

If we make it to heaven, Jesus will give us his eternal science.

If we make it to heaven, Jesus will give us eternal discoveries.

If we make it to heaven, Jesus will give us eternal truth.

If we make it to heaven, Jesus will give us eternal astronomy.

If we make it to heaven, Jesus will give us eternal food to eat from the tree of life.

If we make it to heaven, Jesus will give us eternal health.

If we make it to heaven, Jesus will give us eternal youth.

If we make it to heaven, Jesus will give us eternal prosperity.

If we make it to heaven, Jesus will give us eternal eyes to see.

If we make it to heaven, Jesus will give us eternal ears to hear.

If we make it to heaven, Jesus will give us eternal hands.

If we make it to heaven, Jesus will give us eternal arms.

If we make it to heaven, Jesus will give us eternal legs.

If we make it to heaven, Jesus will give us eternal feet.

If we make it to heaven, Jesus will give us eternal good hygiene.

If we make it to heaven, Jesus will give us an eternal memory.

If we make it to heaven, Jesus will give us eternal love.

If we make it to heaven, Jesus will give us eternal humility.

If we make it to heaven, Jesus will give us eternal trust in Him.

If we make it to heaven, Jesus will give us eternal holiness.

If we make it to heaven, Jesus will give us eternal righteousness.

If we make it to heaven, Jesus will give us eternal perfection.

If we make it to heaven, Jesus will give us eternal life.

If we make it to heaven, everything that we get from Jesus will be eternal.

If we make it to heaven, Jesus will give us an eternal heart.

If we make it to heaven, Jesus will give us eternal joy.

If we make it to heaven, Jesus will give us eternal peace.

If we make it to heaven, Jesus will give us eternal temperance.

If we make it to heaven, Jesus will give us eternal wisdom.

If we make it to heaven, Jesus will give us eternal knowledge.

If we make it to heaven, Jesus will give us eternal faith in Him.

If we make it to heaven, Jesus will give us eternal spiritual things.

If we make it to heaven, Jesus will give us an eternal education.

There are so many more things that Jesus will give to us.

If we make it to heaven, we will be so happy that we made it to heaven only through Jesus Christ who is coming back again to take us to heaven if we are saved in Him.

If we make it to heaven, Jesus will give us eternal things that may baffle us, but we will be very cheerful to receive eternal supernatural things from the Lord if we are saved in Him.

Jesus will take us back to heaven when He comes back again with all of His angels up in the sky.

Education

There are people who love to show off their education.

They will show off by speaking big fancy words that can't be understood by those who are uneducated.

It's a blessing from the Lord to get a good education but don't show off your education by causing uneducated people to feel dumb.

Use your education to bless people by being down to earth and speaking in a simple fashion.

College is not for everybody to go to and get a good education.

A good education is meant to be used to help the poor and needy to better their circumstances, which can't happen when you speak down to them.

Getting a good education is not about speaking big fancy words to make yourself look good, especially before those who are not educated.

Nobody can ever be more educated than Jesus Christ, who spoke in a down to earth way without sin.

Jesus never spoke big fancy words even though He could have done that, because Jesus is the educator of the heavens and other worlds.

Jesus is the educator of educators and no educated person knows how to come down to earth and speak plain and simple words to you and me better than Jesus.

There are people who are so educated that they have a hard time being down to earth and speaking plain and simple words.

The Pharisees and religious leaders could never outsmart Jesus with their limited education that they believed to be superb in their own eyes.

Jesus was all-knowing, and knew what they would say before they spoke one word.

There are people who love to flaunt their education to look so important, especially in the eyes of uneducated people who no one can educate better than Jesus.

Jesus can surely educate simple people with His wisdom so they have good common sense to make good choices every day.

There are some educated fools who make bad choices every day.

Jesus educated us the most through His holy word because there is no higher education above God's holy word for us to live by day after day.

Getting a college education is a good thing, but it does not guarantee to make us wise; there are educated people who do foolish things.

There are people who are very well educated in God's word that has elevated, sharpened, enhanced and enriched their minds for them to do extraordinary things in their lives.

God the Father, the Son and the Holy Spirit educated all eternity for the angels and other worlds to forever know that God is all-wise and all-knowing beyond the limited education of human begins who were born in sin to die and know nothing.

Lower Than

Jesus came down lower than any sinner when He hung on the cross that made Him become sin in our place.

Jesus came down lower than any sinner when His heavenly Father, God, turned His back on Him causing him to ask, "Why hast thou forsaken me?"

It was too hard for God to see His only begotten Son becoming sin on the cross and dying on the cross in our place.

You and I have no excuse to believe that Jesus doesn't know what we are going through in our lives.

You and I have no excuse to believe that Jesus doesn't understand our hardships.

You and I have no excuse to believe that Jesus never felt all the emotions we've felt.

You and I have no excuse to believe that Jesus can't bring us through anything because nothing is too hard for Jesus.

No one has any excuse to believe that their sins are too many for Jesus not to cleanse them of and save them from their sins.

No one has the excuse to believe that their sins are too bad for Jesus not to cleanse them of and save them from their sins.

Jesus came down lower than any sinner when He hung on the cross and become sin in our place to save us from our sins.

Jesus rose from the grave with the victory over the worst kind of sin called death, being the worst kind as a result of our sins.

No one is too much of a sinner that Jesus can't save them from their sins if they confess and repent, which anyone can choose to do.

Jesus chose to give up His life on the cross before He created this world that He came to by choosing to live among sinners like you and me.

No one can believe that they are too low down of a sinner that Jesus can't save them from being lost in their sins.

Jesus became our sins on the cross to become so much lower than any sinner.

If anyone is lost in their sins, they can't tell God on judgement day that they didn't have a choice to choose to believe in His Son, Jesus Christ, and be saved.

Jesus made it possible for even the worst sinner to be saved in Him who died on the cross and rose from the grave.

No sinner has ever come down lower than Jesus who became sin on the cross in our place.

Jesus became sin and took on every sin that no one could ever bear because there are too many and it is too hard for us.

Jesus came down lower than any sinner, when He was on the cross.

Eternity witnessed this and walked away with tears rolling down its cheeks.

God loved the world, so He gave His only begotten Son so whosoever believeth in Him shall not perish but shall have eternal life.

Who Can Know the Heart?

Who can know the heart that can have many prison cells?
Who can know the heart that can have many locked doors?
Who can know the heart that can have many worn out shoes?
Who can know the heart that can have many dirty clothes?
Who can know the heart that can have many molds?
Who can know the heart that can have many sinkholes?
Who can know the heart that can have many mudslides?
Who can know the heart that can have many volcano eruptions?
Who can know the heart that can have many potholes?
Who can know the heart that can have many bits of mildew?
Who can know the heart that can have many weeds?
Who can know the heart that can have many dents?
Who can know the heart that can have many wrecks?
Who can know the heart that can have many broke pieces of glass?
Who can know the heart that can have many wrinkles?
Who can know the heart that can have many blowout tires?
Who can know the heart that can have many broken chairs?
Who can know the heart that can have many earthquakes?
Who can know the heart that can have many tornadoes?
Who can know the heart that can have many hurricanes?
Who can know the heart that can have many floods?
Who can know the heart that can have many heatwaves?
Who can know the heart that can have many wildfires?
Who can know the heart that can have many tidal waves?

Who can know the heart that can have many ashes?

Who can know the heart that Jesus will not condemn?

Who can know the heart that Jesus knows completely?

Who can know the heart that Jesus loves to renew?

Who can know the heart that Jesus wants to dwell in?

Who can know the heart that Jesus wants to love Him?

Who can know the heart that needs the love of Jesus?

Who can know the heart that is empty without Jesus in it?

Who can know the heart that only Jesus can judge?

Who can know the heart that only Jesus can truly understand?

Who can know the heart that only Jesus can save from sin?

Who can know the heart that only Jesus can cleanse from sin?

Who can know the heart that chooses its destiny?

Who can know the heart that only Jesus truly knows is destined for heaven or hell?

Are Better Than

Only you, O Lord, are better than anyone else.

Only you, O Lord, are worthy to be better than anyone else because You, O Lord, were the holy human being who lived in this world without sin.

No human being is better than any other human being because every human being was born in sin except You, my Lord and Savior Jesus Christ.

You were the only human being who didn't sin against God.

O Lord, You were the Son of God and were born in this world through a virgin teenage girl who God filled with His Holy Spirit for You to be born without sin in your flesh.

O Lord, You were born of the Holy Spirit out of the womb of a virgin teenage girl to be better than any other human being who ever lived in this world.

Only You, O Lord, are better than any human being who is alive today.

Only You, O Lord are worthy to be better than any future human being to be born in this world and live in this world only to be saved in You for confessing and repenting of sins unto You who are worthy to be the Savior of the world.

O Lord, I truly know that this world has many sinful human beings who believe that they are better than other sinful human beings because they have more money or more possessions, but they can't take those to the grave with them.

Many sinful human beings believe that they are better than other sinful human beings because their skin's complexion is lighter or they are smarter.

Only You, my Lord Jesus Christ, are worthy to be better because only You were born in this world without sin.

Only You, O Lord, lived in this world without ever sinning against God.

Only You, O Lord, are worthy for all angels and humans to bow down unto You and worship You, who is also better than all the angels in heaven.

Many sinful human beings believe that they are better than other sinful human beings because they are bigger and taller and look better.

Only the Lord Jesus Christ was a sinless human being and worthy of everyone's praise every day.

Only Jesus is better than every human being who ever lived and is alive today.

The Truth Can Heal Anyone

The truth can heal anyone from the deep cuts of lies.

The truth can heal anyone from the sores of lies.

The truth can heal anyone from the blisters of lies.

The truth can heal anyone from the wounds of lies.

The truth can heal anyone from the pain of lies.

The truth can heal anyone from the viruses of lies.

The truth can heal anyone from the sicknesses of lies.

The truth can heal anyone from the diseases of lies.

The truth can heal anyone from the broken bones of lies.

The truth can heal anyone from the fractured ribs of lies.

The truth can heal anyone from the cancer of lies.

The truth can heal anyone from the diabetes of lies.

The truth can heal anyone from the depression of lies.

The truth can heal anyone from the acne of lies.

The truth can heal anyone from the insomnia of lies.

The truth can heal anyone from the shingles of lies.

The truth can heal anyone from the Alzheimer's of lies.

The truth can heal anyone from the bipolar of lies.

The truth can heal anyone from the schizophrenia of lies.

The truth can heal anyone from the glaucoma of lies.

The truth can heal anyone from the cataracts of lies.

The truth is healing, spiritual medicine from the Lord Jesus Christ who is the way, the truth and the life.

The truth is healing power to set us free from lies.

The truth can heal anyone from the flu of lies.

The truth can heal anyone from the coronavirus of lies.

The truth can heal anyone from the pneumonia of lies.

The truth doesn't make anyone ill for loving the truth and living the truth of God's holy word.

O Lord, You Brought Me

O Lord, You brought me through the dark tunnels in my life.

O Lord, You brought me through the dark caves in my life.

O Lord, You brought me through the storms in my life.

O Lord, You brought me through the hurricanes in my life.

O Lord, You brought me through the tornadoes in my life.

O Lord, You brought me through the tidal waves in my life.

O Lord, You brought me through the flood waters in my life.

O Lord, You brought me through the wildfires in my life.

O Lord, You brought me through the unpredictability in my life.

O Lord, You brought me through the car crashes in my life.

O Lord, You brought me through the heat waves in my life.

O Lord, You brought me through the lion's den in my life.

O Lord, You brought me through the snow blizzards in my life.

O Lord, You brought me from a mighty long ways in my life.

O Lord, You brought me through the frost bites in my life.

O Lord, You brought me through the trench foots in my life.

O Lord, You brought me through the spider bites in my life.

O Lord, You brought me through the viruses in my life.

O Lord, You brought me through the heartaches in my life.

O Lord, You brought me through the tears in my life.

O Lord, You brought me through the wrinkles in my life.

O Lord, You brought me through the sores in my life.

O Lord, You brought me through the broken glass in my life.

O Lord, You brought me through the failures in my life.

O Lord, You brought me through the hopelessness in my life.

O Lord, You brought me through the defeats in my life.

O Lord, You brought me through the droughts in my life.

O Lord, You brought me through the famines in my life.

O Lord, You brought me from a mighty long ways in my life.

O Lord, You brought me through the rain forests in my life.

O Lord, You brought me through the insomnia in my life.

O Lord, You brought me through the earthquakes in my life.

O Lord, You brought me through the tsunamis in my life.

O Lord, You brought me from a mighty long ways that takes my mind up into Your miraculous spiritual heights and lets me know that I didn't bring myself this far to see this day that I don't deserve to see no matter what good things that I do.

Strayed Away from the Lord

If you have strayed away from the Lord, the devil doesn't want you to come back to the Lord.

The devil will try his best to keep you from coming back to the Lord.

If you have strayed away from the Lord, the devil will tempt you with a high-paying job to keep you from coming back to the Lord.

If you have strayed away from the Lord, the devil will tempt you with a boyfriend to keep you from coming back to the Lord.

If you have strayed away from the Lord, the devil will tempt you with a girlfriend to keep you from coming back to the Lord.

If you have strayed away from the Lord, the devil will tempt you with living in pleasure to keep you from coming back to the Lord.

If you have strayed away from the Lord, the devil will tempt you with guilt to keep you from coming back to the Lord.

If you have strayed away from the Lord, the devil will tempt you with unforgiveness to keep you from coming back to the Lord.

If you have strayed away from the Lord, the devil will tempt you with pride to keep you from coming back to the Lord.

If you have strayed away from the Lord, the devil will tempt you with prosperity to keep you from coming back to the Lord.

If you have strayed away from the Lord, the devil will tempt you with possessions to keep you from coming back to the Lord.

If you have strayed away from the Lord, the devil will tempt you with wealth to keep you from coming back to the Lord.

If you have strayed away from the Lord, the devil will tempt you with foolishness to keep you from coming back to the Lord.

If you have strayed away from the Lord, the devil will tempt you with deceit to keep you from coming back to the Lord.

If you have strayed away from the Lord, the devil will tempt you with his lies to keep you from coming back to the Lord.

If you have strayed away from the Lord, the devil will tempt you with fame to keep you from coming back to the Lord.

If you have strayed away from the Lord, the devil will tempt you with complacency to keep you from coming back to the Lord.

If you have strayed away from the Lord, the devil will tempt you with not a care in this world to keep you from coming back to the Lord.

If you have strayed away from the Lord, the devil will tempt you with believing you are self-made to keep you from coming back to the Lord.

If you have strayed away from the Lord, the devil will tempt you with selfishness to keep you from coming back to the Lord.

The devil doesn't want you to come back to the Lord, who will be so joyful to receive you back to Him no matter what bad things you have done.

If you confess and repent of your sins and come back to the Lord, you will receive a clean slate and all the wrongs you did will be wiped away.

The Lord will cast your sins to the bottom of the sea.

If you come back to the Lord with all of your heart, the Lord will make the devil flee away from you and he will have no power over you anymore.

Back Up into Our Faces

There are people who will throw our past life back up into our faces, especially if they think you and I will rise up above them.

There are people who won't let us forget how we used to be in our past lives.

There are people who will throw our past lives back up into our faces, especially if they see that the Lord is blessing you and me really well in our present lives.

There are people who don't want to see you and me do better in our lives if they are not doing better in their lives.

There are people who will hold our past mistakes against us as if they have never done anything bad and believe they are better than you and me, and they'll throw our past lives back up into our faces.

There are people who will try to keep you and me down under them with their high-minded, proud ways because they believe that they deserve to do better than you and me in life.

The Lord Jesus Christ shows no respect of persons in who He will truly bless for loving Him and keeping His Commandments.

Jesus doesn't look back at anyone's past life and throw that past life back up into their faces.

Jesus is all about improving our lives to do His holy will, no matter what bad things that you or I did in our past lives.

If anyone throws our past life back into our faces, then Jesus will throw their past lives back up into their faces no matter how well off they are in their lives.

Nobody would want Jesus to throw their past life back up into their face because they wouldn't be able to handle it when they see their past sins hunting them down like a ghost.

It's never wise to throw a child of God's past life back up into his or her face because if we do that, God will throw our past lives back up into our faces for you and me to truly see that we haven't been transformed into newness of life to be like Jesus Christ, who will erase our past sinful life if we are saved in him.

Many People Don't Talk About Jesus

Many people will talk about who they see.
Many people will talk about how they feel.
Many people will talk about what they did.
Many people will talk about what they can do.
Many people don't talk about Jesus.
Many people will talk about their car.
Many people will talk about their truck.
Many people will talk about their pets.
Many people will talk about their success.
Many people will talk about their job.
Many people don't talk about Jesus.
Many people will talk about their education.
Many people will talk about their children.
Many people will talk about their spouse.
Many people will talk about sports.
Many people will talk about where they've been.
Many people will talk about where they want to go.
Many people will talk about how many awards they have.
Many people will talk about how many trophies they have.
Many people will talk about their problems.
Many people don't talk about Jesus.
Many people will talk about how much money they make.

Many people will talk about what they heard.
Many people will talk about the news.
Many people will talk about politics.
Many people will talk about technology.
Many people will talk about science.
Many people don't talk about Jesus.
Many people will talk about food.
Many people will talk about clothes.
Many people will talk about jewelry.
Many people will talk about makeup.
Many people will talk about hairstyles.
Many people don't talk about Jesus.
Many people will talk about movie stars.
Many people will talk about entertainers.
Many people will talk about the government.
Many people don't talk about Jesus.
Many people will talk about crimes.
Many people will talk about romance.
Many people will talk about sex.
Many people will talk about luck.
Many people will talk about magic.
Many people will talk about nature.
Many people don't talk about Jesus.
Many people will talk about history.
Many people will talk about human beings.
Many people will talk about their talents.

Many people will talk about their skills.

Many people will talk about the military.

Many people will talk about war.

Many people will talk about their prosperity.

Many people will talk about their poverty.

Many people don't talk about Jesus.

Many people will talk about who treated them bad.

Many people will talk about what they want to do.

Many people will talk about who they helped.

Many people will talk about what they have.

Many people will talk about what they believe.

Many people will talk about the weather.

Many people will talk about climate change.

Many people will talk about horoscopes.

Many people will talk about their health.

Many people will talk about their rights.

Many people don't talk about Jesus.

Many people will talk about injustice.

Many people will talk about their accomplishments.

Many people will talk about their pride.

Many people will talk about their mistakes.

Many people will talk about their loved ones.

Many people will talk about their friends.

Many people will talk about their life.

Many people will talk about death.

Many people will talk about their enemies.

Many people don't talk about Jesus Christ who talks about us human beings to His heavenly Father God up in the heavenly courtroom where Jesus is pleading our cases before God.

Many people don't talk about Jesus who gives us all life, health and strength, which we can take for granted.

Many people don't talk about Jesus who blesses us all, even when we mistake His blessings for our own belief that we are self-made and caused our own prosperity.

Many people don't talk about Jesus Christ who is the head of the church.

Many church folks don't talk about Jesus much at all to the people of the world.

Many people will talk about things that have no substance like air.

Jesus will talk to us in His holy words that give us the full description of the greatest and most powerful words of truth for us all to live by every day.

There is eternal, holy, righteous and divine substance in Jesus' talk.

Many people will talk about everybody else except Jesus.

Many people will talk about everything else except Jesus Christ who every real, true Christian loves to talk about and loves to obey.

God Will Not Change His Holy Word

The seasons will change, but God will not change His holy word.

Our moods can change, but God will not change His holy word.

Our behavior can change, but God will not change His holy word.

Our voices can change, but God will not change His holy word.

Our feelings can change, but God will not change His holy word.

We can change our minds, but God will not change His holy word.

We can change our clothes, but God will not change His holy word.

The wind can change and blow in a different direction, but God will not change His holy word.

We can change our plans, but God will not change His holy word.

Our lives can change, but God will not change His holy word.

Time will change, but God will not change His holy word.

We can go through changes in our lives, but God will not change His holy word.

Our bodies can change, but God will not change His holy word.

We can change what we say, but God will not change His holy word.

This world will change, but God will not change His holy word.

God will not change the truth of His holy word.

The heavens and earth will pass away before God would change His holy word.

Technology can change, but God will not change His holy word.

Science can change, but God will not change His holy word.

Luck can change, but God will not change His holy word.

People can change, but God will not change His holy word.

All existence would disappear before God would change His holy word.

We can change our theories, but God will not change His holy word.

We can change the way we look, but God will not change His holy word.

God will not change His holy word for anyone, no matter how rich and great they are.

God will not change His holy word that is all about God sending His only begotten Son, Jesus Christ, to this sinful world to redeem all human beings back to God.

God had predestined His holy word to never change, even before God created the angels in heaven.

No fallen angel and no human being can change God's holy word that didn't change in the Garden of Eden where Adam and Eve's lives changed from total perfection to totally flawed in sin for disobeying God who spoke the truth of His holy word to them to live by in the Garden of Eden.

It Doesn't Take Much at All

It doesn't take much at all to get into an accident.

It doesn't take much at all to fall down.

It doesn't take much at all to forget something.

It doesn't take much at all to get sick.

It doesn't take much at all to get disappointed.

It doesn't take much at all to say something wrong.

It doesn't take much at all to feel bad.

It doesn't take much at all to feel proud.

It doesn't take much at all to get hurt.

It doesn't take much at all to make a mistake.

It doesn't take much at all to get angry.

It doesn't take much at all to think wrong.

It doesn't take much at all to be selfish.

It doesn't take much at all to not see one's own flaws.

It doesn't take much at all to not see one's own sins.

It doesn't take much at all to quench the Holy Spirit.

It doesn't take much at all to deny Jesus Christ.

It doesn't take much at all to sin against God.

It doesn't take much at all to doubt what Jesus can do for us.

It doesn't take much at all to be lost in our sins.

It doesn't take much at all to choose to do right or wrong.

It doesn't take much at all to lie to oneself.

It doesn't take much at all to live a lie.

It doesn't take much at all to die.

It doesn't take much at all for Jesus to save us from our sins if we confess and repent and turn away from our sins.

It doesn't take much at all for Jesus to give anyone a second chance to deny self and pick up one's cross and follow Him before it's too late.

There is Nothing

There is nothing right about thinking wrong.

There is nothing right about talking wrong.

There is nothing right about doing wrong.

There is nothing wrong about thinking right.

There is nothing wrong about talking right.

There is nothing wrong about doing right.

You and I don't know everything that is right.

You and I don't know everything that is wrong.

There is nothing right about thinking bad thoughts.

There is nothing right about saying bad words.

There is nothing right about doing bad things.

There is nothing wrong about thinking good thoughts.

There is nothing wrong about saying good words.

There is nothing wrong about doing good things.

If we want to know everything that is right, we can study the bible because it will let us know everything that is right.

If we want to know everything that is wrong, we can study the bible because it will let us know everything that is wrong.

There is nothing right that is left out of the bible.

There is nothing wrong that is left out of the bible.

There is nothing right about rejecting Jesus.

There is nothing wrong about believing in Jesus Christ.

There is nothing right about breaking God's Commandments.

There is nothing wrong about keeping God's Commandments.

There is nothing right about turning one's back on Jesus.

There is nothing wrong about holding onto Jesus.

There is nothing right about being of the world.

There is nothing wrong about being like Jesus.

There is nothing right about being lost in our sins.

There is nothing wrong about being saved in Jesus Christ.

There is nothing right about worshipping the devil.

There is nothing wrong about worshipping Jesus Christ.

There is nothing right about going to hell.

There is nothing wrong about going to heaven.

There is nothing right about not going to church.

There is nothing wrong about going to church.

There is nothing right about hating anyone.

There is nothing wrong about loving everybody.

There is nothing right about quenching the Holy Spirit.

There is nothing wrong about obeying the voice of the Holy Spirit.

There is nothing right about believing that there is no God.

There is nothing wrong about believing in an unseen God.

If We Go

If we go in the wrong direction for the love of money, Jesus won't be there.

If we go in the wrong direction of living in pleasure, Jesus won't be there.

If we go in the wrong direction of knowing what is right and not doing right, Jesus won't be there.

If we go in the wrong direction of telling lies, Jesus won't be there.

If we go in the wrong direction of showing respect of persons, Jesus won't be there.

If we go in the wrong direction of gossiping, Jesus won't be there.

If we go in the wrong direction of being proud, Jesus won't be there.

If we go in the wrong direction of being selfish, Jesus won't be there.

If we go in the wrong direction of disunity in the church, Jesus won't be there.

If we go in the right direction of returning faithful tithes and offerings, Jesus will be there.

If we go in the right direction of having faith in Jesus, Jesus will be there.

If we go in the right direction of trusting Jesus, Jesus will be there.

If we go in the right direction of being humble unto Jesus, Jesus will be there.

If we go in the right direction of loving everybody, Jesus will be there.

If we go in the right direction of being selfless, Jesus will be there.

If we go in the right direction of loving Jesus, Jesus will be there.

If we go in the right direction of keeping God's Commandments, Jesus will be there.

If we go in the right direction of confessing and repenting of our sins unto Jesus, Jesus will be there.

If we go in the right direction of being a witness for Jesus, Jesus will be there.

If we go in the right direction of giving testimonies about what Jesus brought us through, Jesus will be there.

If we go in the right direction of not denying Jesus before anyone, Jesus will be there.

If we go in the right direction of spreading the good news about Jesus Christ, Jesus will be there with you and me in spirit and truth.

If we go in the right direction of giving Jesus all the glory and praise, Jesus will be there.

If we go in the right direction of giving Jesus our all, Jesus will be there with us in the right direction that leads us to Him every day.

If we go in the right direction of studying God's holy word, Jesus will be there.

If we go in the right direction of living by God's holy word, Jesus will be there.

If we go in the right direction of praying without ceasing, Jesus will be there.

If we go in the right direction of doing God's holy will and not our own will, Jesus will be there because Jesus did His heavenly father's holy will when Jesus lived here on earth.

If we go in the right direction of keeping our eyes on Jesus, Jesus will be there.

If we go in the right direction of obeying the voice of God's Holy Spirit, Jesus will be there.

If we go in the right direction of forgiving others who have done us wrong, Jesus will be there.

Jesus will also give us the strength to keep our distance from those who want to keep on doing us wrong.

Many People Don't

Many people don't believe in Jesus Christ because they believe in the things in this world.

Many people don't put their trust in Jesus Christ because they put their trust in the things in this world.

Many people don't love Jesus Christ because they love the things in this world.

Many people don't believe that Jesus can do anything for them because they believe that they are self-made.

Many people don't believe that Jesus can give them the victory over their struggles because they believe that they can get the victory over their struggles.

Many people don't pray to Jesus about their problems because they believe that they can work out their own problems.

Many people in church don't put their faith in Jesus because they believe that who they see or what they see can fulfill their life.

Many people even in the church don't keep Jesus' ten Commandments because they believe that the Commandments have nothing to do with their daily walk with Jesus.

Many people in the church don't believe that Jesus is a miracle worker because they believe in ordinary things that have numbed their senses and limited their faith in Jesus.

Many people in the church don't believe in Jesus Christ because they believe in themselves and think they don't have any sins to confess and repent of.

Many people in this world don't want to believe that there is a God because they believe that Christians are hypocrites and believe that the bible is a fairy tale book.

Many people in this world don't believe that there is a devil because they believe that whatever bad things happen are meant to happen for no reason, when it's the devil that's the reason for bad things that happen to anyone.

Many people don't believe they will go to hell because they believe that God will excuse them from living in their sins.

Many people in this world don't believe that Jesus Christ is coming back again because they believe that we Christians are wasting our time going to church as they see many church folks leaving the church.

Many people don't believe in Jesus Christ because they believe that this world can put them in a heaven and that everything they are doing in their lives is all right, but God will close probation on this world for Jesus to stand up and say that it is finished.

Pure Works Unto the Lord

Pure works unto the Lord means helping those who are in need to glorify the Lord and not to help someone to make themselves look good.

Pure works unto the Lord means being there for our spiritual brothers and sisters when they are going through hard times in their lives.

Pure works unto the Lord means pure actions with no selfish motives and intentions to want to draw attention to yourself for doing good things for others.

We can have all the faith that we want in the Lord, but if our works are not pure and from our hearts, we will have no favor from the Lord no matter how much favor we get from people.

The Lord truly knows if our works are pure with no hidden secret pride involved.

We can't hide from the Lord who will sooner or later reveal our true identity, motives and intentions to others who will see that our actions are not pure and about glorifying Jesus' holy name.

Pure works unto the Lord go hand in hand with our faith in the Lord because how can we believe in Jesus Christ and have no pure works and pure actions to show that whatever we do is to glorify the Lord and not to exalt ourselves?

Pure works unto the Lord are only for the Lord to always know because the Lord knows our deep, inner reasons and thoughts that no one but Him can see.

Outward appearance of works can look so pure and holy, but the heart can be corrupt with impure motives and intentions.

We need to always pray and ask the Lord to help us to have pure works, since that is proof that we believe in Jesus Christ whose works were always pure unto God when He lived on earth without sin

O Lord, Help Me

O Lord, help me to live right by the truth of Your holy word.

I know, O Lord, You give me Your holy spirit to help me to remember what I need to know about You, my Lord and Savior Jesus Christ.

O Lord, my soul cries out for Your help that I need twenty-four hours around the clock.

O Lord, help me not to take even one second of Your love, mercy and grace for granted as if I am self-made and don't need You.

O Lord, help me to love you with all of my mind, heart, soul and strength that is always good for me to do.

I don't have to feel insecure, because You, O Lord, will always be there for me on my good days and bad days.

O Lord, help me to always know that I didn't bring myself this far in my life, because it's You who has brought me this far in my life.

O Lord, help me to give You my all.

I know I don't have to worry about whether my all is good enough to please you, O Lord, because You always know the limit of my all.

Only You can judge when my all may not be good enough; human beings can't judge this.

O Lord, help me to listen to and obey the voice of Your holy spirit who will lead and guide me into all the truth about You, my Lord and Savior Jesus Christ.

O Lord, help me to love everybody and to treat everybody right, even my enemies who can't do more harm to me that what You allow.

O Lord, help me to fully trust You and not trust me, who is not perfect and makes mistakes.

O Lord, help me to live my life unto You, who gives life its true meaning to exist beyond death that is only temporary.

You, O Lord, are the eternal life to give to me for being saved in You, O Lord

How We Grew Up

How we grew up has a lot to do with how we are today.

Some things in us are just hereditary and were passed down to us from our parents and grandparents.

We have some habits that were passed down to us from our parents and grandparents and maybe even from our great-grandparents.

How we grew up has a lot to do with how we live our lives.

How we grew up has a lot to do with how we make our choices today.

No one grew up in a perfect family, no matter how rich you are.

No one grew up in a perfect family, no matter how educated you are.

No one grew up in a perfect family, no matter how genius you are.

How we grew up has a lot to do with how we will end up in life.

Thanks to Jesus Christ, how we grew up can't cause us to be lost in our sins, if we confess and repent of our sins unto Jesus Christ who gave up His life on the cross and rose from the grave to save us from our sins and give us eternal life when He comes back again.

How we grew up has a lot to do with how far we will go in life, but thanks to Jesus Christ, all things are possible through Him who can bless us to go very far in life no matter how we grew up.

Just Because We

Just because we go to church it doesn't mean that everything will be smooth all the time.

Just because we worship the Lord doesn't mean that everything will be smooth all the time.

Just because we are working for the Lord doesn't mean that everything will be smooth all the time.

Just because we have a relationship with the Lord doesn't mean that everything will be smooth all the time.

Just because we hold office positions in the church doesn't mean that everything will be smooth all the time.

Just because we have spiritual gifts in the church doesn't mean that everything will be smooth all the time.

Just because we pray to the Lord doesn't mean that everything will be smooth all the time.

Just because we are blessed by the Lord doesn't mean that everything will be smooth all the time.

Just because we return faithful tithes and offerings doesn't mean that everything will be smooth all the time.

Just because we read the bible doesn't mean that everything will be smooth all the time.

Just because we have faith in the Lord Jesus Christ doesn't mean that everything will be smooth all the time.

Just because we love Jesus and keep His Commandments doesn't mean that everything will be smooth all the time.

Just because we confess and repents of our sins unto the Lord doesn't mean that everything will be smooth all the time.

Just because we are saved in Jesus Christ doesn't mean that everything will be smooth all the time.

When Jesus lived here on earth without sin everything wasn't smooth all the time for Him.

Jesus had many rough times.

Every day, the devil tried to cause Jesus to sin against God.

The devil used every temptation he had to try to cause Jesus to fail His great mission from God, but Jesus got the victory overall the devil's temptations.

Living Our Life Unto the Lord

Living our life unto the Lord is believing in the Lord Jesus Christ, even if we are on our death bed.

Living our life unto the Lord is submitting ourselves to the Holy Spirit who will lead and guide us into all the truth to set us free from the devil who lies about the Lord.

Living our life unto the Lord is denying ourselves and picking up our crosses to follow the Lord Jesus Christ every day.

Living our life unto the Lord is to humble ourselves unto the Lord Jesus Christ for everything that He does for us because we can't do anything good without Jesus.

Living our life unto the Lord is trusting Jesus to work out our problems that stress us out if we try to work them out on our own.

Living our life unto the Lord is loving the Lord Jesus Christ so much more than loving anyone else who doesn't have a heaven to put us in; only Jesus can do that when He comes back again.

Living our life unto the Lord is confessing and repenting of our sins that the Commandmens make us aware of so we know our sins and are not ignorant.

Living our life unto the Lord is going through some trials to help us to be about the Lord Jesus Christ's business every day that the Lord gives us the strength to represent Him in our trials for His holy name's sake.

Living our life unto the Lord is a free will choice of obedience that we fall short of in some kind of way every day that the Lord reaches out to us with His love, mercy and grace to bring us back to Him who we stray away from in some kind of way and don't see it.

Living our life unto the Lord is a lifetime of being more and more like Jesus, who we can't be like without the Holy Spirit living in us day by day.

Living our life unto the Lord is living a life of holy divine action that will convince unbelievers to believe in Jesus Christ more than quoting the bible scriptures to them.

Jesus is more seen in action than in words which can be full of hot air coming out of our mouths and going nowhere to not build up the church.

Only the Lord is Always Right

Only the Lord is always right about everything.
Only the Lord is always right about everybody.
We are not always right about what we think.
We are not always right about what we say.
We are not always right about what we feel.
We are not always right about what we do.
We are not always right about the choices that we make.
Only the Lord is always right about all things.
The Lord is never wrong about anything.
The Lord is never wrong about anybody.
The Lord is never wrong about what He says.
The Lord is never wrong about what He can do.
We can say something wrong.
We ca think something wrong.
We can do something wrong.
We can feel something wrong.
Only the Lord is always right when we can be so wrong.
Only the Lord is always right when our motives can be so wrong.
Only the Lord is always right when our intentions can be so wrong.
Only the Lord is always right when our ideas can be so wrong.
Only the Lord is always right when our feelings can be so wrong.
Only the Lord is always right when our thoughts can be so wrong.
Only the Lord is always right when our desires can be so wrong.
Only the Lord is always right when our goals can be so wrong.

Only the Lord is always and forever right in His holy word.

Only the Lord is always and forever right beyond our life that is short-lived in God's eternal eyesight.

Only the Lord is always and forever right when our lives will be so wrong if we don't live our lives unto the Lord.

The Knowledge of God

Many of us grew up only learning about the knowledge of the world.

The knowledge of the world filled up the textbooks that we were required to read in kindergarten, middle school and high school.

Many of us only knew about the material things in this world that will one day pass away, but we didn't know that because it wasn't written down in the textbooks.

Many of us grew up only learning many things about sinful human beings.

Many of us didn't learn anything about the knowledge of God that is written in His holy words.

The knowledge of God is high above the knowledge of the world that no one can truly stand on day after day.

The knowledge of God will stand forever and ever above the technology in this world that will one day pass away because it won't be of any good use in heaven.

Many of us grew up only learning about the knowledge of the world, and that has kept us from spiritual things that are rooted and grounded in the knowledge of God.

The knowledge of God is eternal in Jesus Christ, who is the word of God for all of the heavens and worlds to know about forever and ever.

In the Everlasting, Loving and Eternal Lord

There is no hate in the everlasting, loving and eternal Lord.

There is no fear in the everlasting, loving and eternal Lord.

There is no lie in the everlasting, loving and eternal Lord.

There is no strife in the everlasting, loving and eternal Lord.

There is no envy in the everlasting, loving and eternal Lord.

There is no division in the everlasting, loving and eternal Lord.

There is no bondage in the everlasting, loving and eternal Lord.

There is no favoritism in the everlasting, loving and eternal Lord.

There is no injustice in the everlasting, loving and eternal Lord.

There is no inequality in the everlasting, loving and eternal Lord.

There is no proudness in the everlasting, loving and eternal Lord.

There is no superiority in the everlasting, loving and eternal Lord.

There is no hopelessness in the everlasting, loving and eternal Lord.

There is no disappointment in the everlasting, loving and eternal Lord.

There is no discouragement in the everlasting, loving and eternal Lord.

There is no failure in the everlasting, loving and eternal Lord.

There is no emptiness in the everlasting, loving and eternal Lord.

There is no sadness in the everlasting, loving and eternal Lord.

There is no defeat in the everlasting, loving and eternal Lord.

There is no discontentment in the everlasting, loving and eternal Lord.

There is no deception in the everlasting loving, and eternal Lord.

There is no bitterness in the everlasting, loving and eternal Lord.

There is no sin in the everlasting, loving and eternal Lord.

There is no eternal death in the everlasting, loving and eternal Lord and Savior, Jesus Christ.

There is no dissatisfaction in the everlasting, loving and eternal Lord.

There is no selfishness in the everlasting, loving and eternal Lord.

There is no doubt in the everlasting, loving and eternal Lord.

There is no insecurity in the everlasting, loving and eternal Lord.

There is no unsupportiveness in the everlasting, loving and eternal Lord.

There is no doom in the everlasting, loving and eternal Lord and Savior, Jesus Christ.

To Anyone Who Loves the Lord

A sermon is not worthless to anyone who loves the Lord.

A gospel is not worthless to anyone who loves the Lord.

A praise poem is not worthless to anyone who loves the Lord.

A testimony is not worthless to anyone who loves the Lord.

A prayer is not worthless to anyone who loves the Lord.

The bible is not worthless to anyone who loves the Lord.

A Christian is not worthless to anyone who loves the Lord.

The church is not worthless to anyone who loves the Lord.

Baptism is not worthless to anyone who loves the Lord.

Conviction is not worthless to anyone who loves the Lord.

Conversion is not worthless to anyone who loves the Lord.

Repentance is not worthless to anyone who loves the Lord.

Obedience is not worthless to anyone who loves the Lord.

Faith is not worthless to anyone who loves the Lord.

Spiritual gifts are not worthless to anyone who loves the Lord.

The Holy Spirit is not worthless to anyone who loves the Lord.

Heaven is not worthless to anyone who loves the Lord.

Eternal life is not worthless to anyone who loves the Lord.

God is not worthless to anyone who loves the Lord.

The devil is worthless to anyone who loves the Lord.

Sin is worthless to anyone who loves the Lord.

Hell is worthless to anyone who loves the Lord

Words are Very Powerful

Words are very powerful because words can have a good effect on us and words can have a bad effect on us.

Words are very powerful because words can build up our self-esteem and words can tear down our self-esteem.

Words are very powerful because words can make us happy and words can make us sad.

Words are very powerful because words can make us laugh and words can make us cry.

Words are very powerful because words can encourage us and words can discourage us.

Words are very powerful because words can make us feel good and words can make us angry.

Words are very powerful because words can be positive and words can be negative.

Words are very powerful because words can heal our heart and words can break our heart.

Words are very powerful because words can be true and words can be lies.

Words are very powerful because words can be loving and words can be hateful.

Words are very powerful because words can make us strong and words can make us weak.

Words are very powerful because words can be straightforward and words can beat around the bush.

Words are very powerful because words can be beautiful and words can be ugly.

Words are very powerful because words can be direct and words can be indirect.

Words are very powerful because words can be victorious and words can be a defeat.

Words are very powerful because words can be exciting and words can be boring.

Words are very powerful because words can prolong our lives and words can shorten our lives.

Words are very powerful because words can be healthy and words can be unhealthy.

Words are very powerful because God's holy word can encourage us to believe in Jesus Christ and the devil's wicked words can discourage us to be lost in our sins.

Words are very powerful because God's holy word is all the truth about Jesus Christ who shed His precious blood and gave up His life on the cross to save us from our sins.

The devil's wicked words are nothing but lies to send us to hell if we believe his lying words.

Words are very powerful because Jesus Christ is the word of God who became flesh and lived without sin among sinners speaking many sinful words against Jesus and only degrading themselves in the presence of God.

Sin Came into this World

Sin came into this world through a man, not through a woman.

A woman was the first to disobey God, but sin came into this world from a man named Adam who knew better than Eve not to even touch that fruit from the tree of knowledge of good and evil.

It was a man who also committed the first murder in this world.

Only we men will go into war with other men.

There has never been a time here on earth where women have gone into war with other women.

There has never been a time here on earth where children have gone into war with other children.

There has never been a time here on earth where animals have gone into war with other animals.

Only us men have gone into war with other men.

We men can truly be the most miserable if we can't have our way.

There was a sinless man who once lived here on earth among sinful men, and He came to redeem sinful men and sinful women back to God.

That sinless man was also the Son of God.

That sinless man was a man of peace, not a man of war.

That sinless man didn't gather an army of men to go to war against His enemies.

That sinless man even humbled himself unto death to save sinful men and sinful women from being lost in sin.

Sin came into this world through one man who knew better than the woman to not disobey God.

Even though there are women who are fighting in a man's war with mostly men fighting in the war, God will hold men accountable for killing especially innocent victims like Cain killed his innocent brother, Abel.

Like a Heavy Downpour of Rain

Problems can come upon us like a heavy downpour, raining disappointments down on us.

Problems can come upon us like a heavy downpour, raining stress down on us.

Problems can come upon us like a heavy downpour, raining pain down on us.

Problems can come upon us like a heavy downpour, raining trouble down on us.

Problems can come upon us like a heavy downpour, raining grief down on us.

Problems can come upon us like a heavy downpour, raining depression down on us.

Problems can come upon us like a heavy downpour, raining sickness down on us.

Problems can come upon us like a heavy downpour, raining discouragement down on us.

Problems can come upon us like a heavy downpour, raining heartache down on us.

Problems can come upon us like a heavy downpour, raining nothing good down on us.

Problems can come upon us like a heavy downpour, raining misfortune down on us.

Problems can come upon us like a heavy downpour, raining lies down on us.

Problems can come upon us like a heavy downpour, raining hate down on us.

Problems can come upon us like a heavy downpour, raining prejudice down on us.

Problems can come upon us like a heavy downpour, raining fear down on us.

Problems can come upon us like a heavy downpour, raining injustice down on us.

Problems can come upon us like a heavy downpour, raining jealousy down on us.

Problems can come upon us like a heavy downpour, raining strife down on us.

Problems can come upon us like a heavy downpour, raining unpredictability down on us.

Problems can come upon us like a heavy downpour, raining uncertainty down on us.

No matter what problems come upon us, we can give them to Jesus who can dry us off with His mercy and grace after we get soaked in our problems.

I Have Some Rascal in Me

I know, O Lord, that I have some rascal in me, but I am so glad that You see some good in me to use me to uplift Your holy name.

I know, O Lord, that I have some rascal in me, but I am so glad that You love me and want to save me from my sins.

I know, O Lord, that I have some rascal in me, but I am so glad that You found me to be fit to deny myself and pick up my cross and follow you.

I know, O Lord, that I have some rascal in me, but I am so glad, O Lord, that You didn't give up on me who was so lost in my sins.

I know, O Lord, that I have some rascal in me, but I am so glad that You brought me this far in my life so a rascal like me can confess and repent of my sins unto You, my Lord and Savior Jesus Christ.

I know, O Lord, that I have some rascal thoughts, but I am so glad that You will enter into my mind for me to think of you, O Lord.

I know, O Lord, that I can say some rascal words, but I am so glad that You will speak through me with Your holy words of everlasting discipline.

I know, O Lord, that I can do some rascal deeds, but I am so glad that You will give me Your holy spirit for me to do right by You.

I know, O Lord, that I have some rascal in me, but I am so glad that You want to cleanse me from my rascal sins and save my soul from being lost in this rascal world.

The Self-Checkout

The purpose of the self-checkout is to check out your own items in the grocery stores.

The self-checkout is usually for people who only have a few items to checkout.

There are people who will be in the self-checkout line with a cart full of food and other items, which holds up the other people waiting in line.

When people are in the self-checkout line with a grocery cart full of food it is not fair to those who only have a few items.

The purpose of the self-checkout is to shorten the long lines of people at the cashier's check-out, but there are people who have a grocery cart full of food going to the self-checkout and causing that line to be too long for people who only have a few items.

No matter what new, good invention someone comes up with, there will be people who will take it for granted and use it in the wrong way to make it hard for others to enjoy using the new, good invention.

There is a spiritual self-checkout for everyone and no one can hold up anyone else in the spiritual self-checkout line of examining themselves so they can be loving and obedient unto the Lord.

It's the Lord who owns all things and surely owns every soul who has a spiritual self-checkout and does not hold up anyone else.

No one in their right mind would not choose to obey the voice of the Holy Spirit leading us into all the truth about Jesus Christ who is the Savior of the world so that all can be saved in Him.

Jesus had a self-checkout in heaven to come to this world at the right time to hasten our destiny to heaven if we are saved in Him.

Jesus has an eternal grocery store in heaven where there are no hold-ups in the self-checkout lines, unlike the self-checkout lines in the grocery stores in this world that can get crowded with people having grocery carts full of food that may not even be good to eat.

Only Jesus Can Cleanse You from Your Sins

Having a good skill can't cleanse you from your sins.

Being a genius can't cleanse you from your sins.

Being educated can't cleanse you from your sins.

Only Jesus can cleanse you from your sins.

Being rich can't cleanse you from your sins.

Being famous can't cleanse you from your sins.

Being beautiful can't cleanse you from your sins.

Only Jesus can cleanse you from your sins.

Being right about what you say can't cleanse you from your sins.

Being talented can't cleanse you from your sins.

Eating the right foods can't cleanse you from your sins.

Only Jesus can cleanse you from your sins.

Dressing in modest apparel can't cleanse you from your sins.

Treating people right can't cleanse you from your sins.

Getting married can't cleanse you from your sins.

Only Jesus can cleanse you from your sins.

Going to church can't cleanse you from your sins.

Holding church positions can't cleanse you from your sins.

Having spiritual gifts in the church can't cleanse you from your sins.

Having big muscles can't cleanse you from your sins.

Being athletic can't cleanse you from your sins.

Only Jesus can cleanse you from your sins.

Being successful can't cleanse you from your sins.

Being a leader can't cleanse you from your sins.

Being great can't cleanse you from your sins.

Only Jesus can cleanse you from your sins and only Jesus can save you from your sins.

There is nothing that we can say and there is nothing that we can to to cleanse ourselves from our sins.

Only Jesus Christ can cleanse you and me from our sins and save us from them if we confess and repent of our sins unto Jesus and turn away from living in our sins.

It's Always Easy for Jesus To

It's not always easy to talk good to someone who talks bad to you.

It's not always easy to be good to someone who isn't good to you.

It's not always easy to treat someone right when he or she doesn't treat you right.

It's not always easy to do something good for someone who doesn't do anything good for you.

It's easy to talk bad to someone who talks bad to you.

It's easy to be bad to someone who is bad to you.

It's easy to do bad things to someone who does bad things to you.

It's not always easy to love someone who doesn't love you.

It's easy to do good things for someone who does good things for you.

It's easy to love someone who loves you.

It's not always easy to deny oneself and pick up one's cross to follow Jesus Christ.

It's always easy for Jesus to save us from our sins if we confess and repent of our sins unto Him.

It's not always easy for us to win souls to Jesus.

It's always easy for Jesus to give us spiritual gifts in the church to win souls for Him.

It's not always easy for us to love everybody the same.

It's always easy for Jesus to love everybody the same because He gave up His life on the cross to save everybody from being lost in their sins.

It's not always easy to get something that we want and need.

It's always easy for Jesus to supply all of our needs and even give us something that we want if it's in His holy will.

It's not always easy to listen to the Holy Spirit telling us to do the right thing.

It's easy to reject the voice of the Holy Spirit and do our own will that can seem to be so right to do.

It's not always easy to make the right choices.

It was easy for the Lord to give us all a free will because the Lord God loves freedom and gave us the freedom to choose freely, whether it's a right or a wrong choice that we can choose every day.

It's not always easy to trust Jesus when all hell breaks loose for you and me.

It's always easy for Jesus to seal us in His saving grace that hell has no power over to cause us to be lost and miss out on heaven that will be easy for Jesus to take us to when He comes back again

Completely Secured

You can only be completely secured in Jesus Christ every day because Jesus is your best security in this world.

You can't be completely secured on your job that can overwork you with a low paying salary.

You can't be completely secured in your house that needs some repair work.

You can't be completely secured in your vehicle that can break down at any moment.

You can only be completely secured in Jesus Christ, who will supply all of your needs.

You can't be completely secured in your money that can be easily spent.

You can't be completely secured in your education that a fool can get and use in the wrong way.

You can't be completely secured in your heart that can get hurt.

You can only be completely secured in Jesus Christ, who will never leave you or forsake you.

You can't be completely secured in your mind that can change.

You can't be completely secured in your marriage that can lack something that you need.

You can't be completely secured in yourself who can make mistakes.

You can only be completely secured in Jesus Christ, who secures your soul to be saved in Him if you confess and repent of your sins and live for Jesus.

You can't be completely secured in your life that can be cut short on any day.

You can't be completely secured in your government that can shut down.

You can't be completely secured in your country that can go to war.

You can't be completely secured in technology that a criminal can use for evil purposes.

You can't be completely secured in this world where natural disasters are rampant.

You and I can only be completely secure in Jesus Christ, who is coming back again to this world to take us to heaven if we are saved in Him who secures all of heaven that wouldn't be heaven without Jesus in it.

You and I can't be completely secured in the church where we can believe that wheat is a tare and a tare is wheat and uproot a wheat because we mistake it for a tare.

You and I can only be completely secured in Jesus Christ, who sees every wheat and every tare in the church to make no mistake about uprooting a tare who can never deceive Jesus who is the head of the church.

We Will Have a Good Time

Many people believe that they are having a good time in this sinful world.

We don't know what a good time is until we make it to heaven.

If we make it to heaven, we will have a good time with all the holy saints forever and ever.

We will have a good time talking to all the holy saints and we will have a good time hanging out with all the holy saints.

We will have a good time talking to all the holy angels and we will have a good time hanging out with all the holy angels.

We will have a good time travelling together to other worlds.

We will have a good time talking to creatures in other worlds and we will have a good time hanging out with the creatures in other worlds.

We will have a good time with our Lord and Savior Jesus Christ.

We will have a good time talking to Jesus face to face.

We will have a good time hanging out with Jesus.

We will have a good time living together in the new earth.

We will have a good time building our houses.

We will have a good time planting our gardens.

We will have a good time living in the countryside in the new earth.

We will have a good time living in the new Jerusalem holy city.

We don't know what a good time is until we live in heaven and live in the new earth.

Many people believe that going to parties is having a good time.

Many people believe that going to concerts is having a good time.

When we get to heaven we will have a holy ghost good time with Jesus and all the holy saints and all the holy angels and with all the other creatures in other worlds forever and ever.

We will have a good time with God forever and ever.

God will fill our hearts with His joy forever and ever.

We will have a good time together in heaven where there will be nothing but love everywhere throughout the heaven and the new earth.

Forever and Ever is Not Long Enough

Forever and ever is not long enough to worship Jesus in His eternal authority.

Forever and ever is not long enough to love Jesus in His eternal love.

Forever and ever is not long enough to uplift Jesus' holy name in His eternal holiness.

Forever and ever is not long enough to live unto Jesus in His eternal righteousness.

Forever and ever is not long enough to testify of Jesus in His eternal Holy Spirit who testifies of Him.

Forever and ever is not long enough to know Jesus in His eternal knowledge of all things in heaven and earth.

Forever and ever is not long enough to work for Jesus in His eternal handiworks of his creations.

Forever and ever is only a glimpse of Jesus' presence in His eternal creations.

Forever and ever is only a moment of Jesus' glory in His eternal existence.

Forever and ever is only a second in His eternal Lordship over all things.

Forever and ever is only a twinkling of an eye in Jesus' eternal perfection.

Forever and ever is not long enough to grasp Jesus' eternal mysteries in other worlds.

Forever and ever is not long enough to learn more and more about Jesus Christ who is the eternal One with God and the Holy Spirit being an eternal learning experience.

Forever and ever will never be long enough to be with Jesus in His eternal life that Jesus will give to all who are saved in Him.

Forever and ever will never be long enough for the saints to live with Jesus in heaven that is only a shadow passing over the landscape without Jesus being there in heaven that Jesus created in His eternal wisdom.

I Never Knew What it was Like

I never knew what it was like to have my father in my life, which had void in it because my father wasn't in my life.

I am sixty-six years old, and today and I still feel the pain from the absence of my father in my life.

One day, I was watching an old western drama on TV about a boy not knowing who his father was until he met his father, who didn't welcome him with open arms right away.

His father was also broken from being in prison for robbing a bank.

The boy and his father finally embraced each other after the boy let his father know how much he missed having his father in his life.

The boy and his father felt the pain from those words spoken by the boy, while at the same time they were set free from the pain when they embraced each other with joy for being relieved from missing each other for years.

When I watched the boy and his father embrace each other, I felt like I wanted to cry because of thinking about my father not being in my life when I was a little boy.

As I grew up into an adult, I finally met my father and talked to him and this gave me great relief from his absence in my life.

My father is deceased now, but I still feel the pain from his absence, especially when I see child actors portraying children who are heartbroken due to the absence of their father in their lives.

I know today that I am so blessed to have a heavenly Father who will never leave me or forsake me.

I just didn't know that God was always with me when I was a child.

I never knew what it was like to have my biological father in my life when I was a child, but today I know what it's like to have my heavenly Father, God, in my life.

Even if my biological father was in my life when I was a child, he would not have been a better father to me than my heavenly Father, God, who no earthly father can out-do in providing for my daily needs.

When I was a Wanderer

When I was a wanderer in my life, O Lord, I am so glad that you didn't give up on me who had no purpose, no focus and no dream in my life.

When I was a wanderer in my life, O Lord, I am so glad that you suffered long for me to know this day that it was You who led me safely through my wanderer's life.

When I was a wanderer in my life, O Lord, I am so glad today that you were there for me every step of the way when I had no sense of direction and didn't know where I was going.

O Lord, I wandered through my life like a lost sheep in the wilderness.

O Lord, I wandered through my life like a little child going out of the house and walking into the street, not realizing the dangers that could befall me.

O Lord, I wandered through my life like the wind blowing in different directions.

O Lord, I wandered through my life like a bubble floating in the air, not knowing where it will land.

When I was a wonderer in my life, O Lord, I am so glad that you didn't leave me helpless in my wandering state of mind that was lost in the abyss of sin.

When I was a wanderer in my life, O Lord, I am so glad that you reached Your almighty hand out to me and pulled me up out of my wandering life that had me on a lockdown for years.

Nobody can tell me, O Lord, that You can't save a wanderer from being lost in sin because You, O Lord, have saved me from being lost.

What I truly know is Your mercy and grace picked me up and carried me through my wandering life like a mother carrying her baby carefully in her arms.

Sometimes, When We Believe

Sometimes, when we believe we are moving forward, we begin to move backwards.

The devil will not let up on us with his temptations, especially tempting us where we are weakest.

You and I must stay in prayer all the time because we might believe we have overcome a weakness, and then it comes back.

It doesn't take much effort to drink something that we shouldn't drink.

It doesn't take much effort to eat something that we shouldn't eat.

It doesn't take much effort to wear something that we shouldn't wear.

It doesn't take much effort to say something that we shouldn't say.

It doesn't take much effort to do something that we shouldn't do.

Sometimes, we can believe that we have gotten the victory over a sin until the devil brings it back to us at full force and all we can do is pray to Jesus to forgive us of that sin and to help us overcome that sin, and Jesus will do just that if we only believe in Him.

Jesus can help our unbelief and strengthen us to move forward as if we never moved backwards.

Sometimes, when we believe that we are moving forward on our spiritual journey towards the Lord, we need to remember that sanctification is a lifetime process for you and me to always need something to overcome in our lives.

Just because we are living for Jesus doesn't mean that we will never sin against Jesus again, which comes to show that confession and repentance is for as long as we live.

For a Display

We put Jesus up for a display if we compromise His holy word with people to please them.

We put Jesus up for a display if we know to do right by the truth of God's holy word and don't do t.

In the bible, Herod's wife, Herodias, wanted the head of John the Baptist, and she got it on a silver platter for a display.

It seems like something that a serial killer would do to display his victims proudly like that.

We put Jesus up for a display if we don't wait on Him to work things out for our faith in Jesus to be questioned.

We put Jesus up for a display to the world if we don't shun the appearance of evil, and instead entertain evil with the knowledge of the truth of God's holy word that we make to look like a lie just so we can fit in with people mixing up the truth with error.

We put Jesus up for a display if we say we are a Christian but we're living in the darkness of sin and put the head of the church on a silver platter of the world to be displayed in our false pretense in the church.

Have Kept Silent

Many churches have kept silent about physical abuse, which means the church is at the tail end and not at the forefront of the evils that are going on in this world.

Many churches have kept silent about sexual abuse, which means the church is at the tail end and not at the forefront of the evils that are going on in this world.

Many churches have kept silent about mental illness, which means the church is at the tail end and not at the forefront of the evils that are going on in this world.

Many churches have kept silent about adultery, which means the church is at the tail end and not at the forefront of the evils that are going on in this world.

Many churches have kept silent about babies being born out of wedlock, which means the church is at the tail end and not at the forefront of the evils that are going on in this world.

Many churches are keeping silent today about what alcohol can do to the mind and body, which means the church is at the tail end and not at the forefront of the evils that are going on in this world.

Many churches are keeping silent today about what drugs can do to the mind and body, which means the church is at the tail end and not at the forefront of the evils that are going on in this world.

Many churches are keeping silent today about Jesus Christ being the Son of God and being one with God, which means the church is at the tail end and not at the forefront of the evils that are going on in this world.

Many churches are keeping silent today about the Holy Spirit who Jesus sent to this world to teach all the truth.

Whoever accepts all the truth and lives all the truth will be at the forefront with Jesus and not at the tail end of the unbelief towards Jesus.

Our Lives Will be Like

Our lives will be like poison if we don't live our lives unto Jesus Christ.

Our lives will be like a disease if we don't live our lives unto Jesus Christ.

Our lives will be like a virus if we don't live our lives unto Jesus Christ.

Our lives will be like rotten fruit if we don't live our lives unto Jesus Christ.

Our lives will be like having Alzheimer if we don't live our lives unto Jesus Christ.

Our lives will be like having dementia if we don't live our lives unto Jesus Christ.

Our lives will be like sewage if we don't live our lives unto Jesus Christ.

Our lives will be like having cancer if we don't live our lives unto Jesus Christ.

Our lives will be like being blind if we don't live our lives unto Jesus Christ.

Our lives will be like being paralyzed if we don't live our lives unto Jesus Christ.

Our lives will be like a toothache if we don't live our lives unto Jesus Christ.

Our lives will be like having arthritis if we don't live our lives unto Jesus Christ.

Our lives will be like having leprosy if we don't live our lives unto Jesus Christ.

Our lives will be like a broken dam if we don't live our lives unto Jesus Christ.

Our lives will be like a mudslide if we don't live our lives unto Jesus Christ.

Our lives will be like a tornado if we don't live our lives unto Jesus Christ.

Our lives will be like a sinking ship if we don't live our lives unto Jesus Christ.

Our lives will be like a wildfire if we don't live our lives unto Jesus Christ.

Our lives will be like quicksand if we don't live our lives unto Jesus Christ.

Our lives will be like a volcano if we don't live our lives unto Jesus Christ.

Our lives will be like a snow blizzard if we don't live our lives unto Jesus Christ.

Our lives will be like bad skunk odor if we don't live our lives unto Jesus Christ.

There is nothing good about not living our lives unto Jesus Christ.

There is nothing right about not living our lives unto Jesus Christ.

There is nothing hopeful about not living our lives unto Jesus Christ.

There is nothing glorious about not living our lives unto Jesus Christ.

There is nothing great about not living our lives unto Jesus Christ.

There is nothing wise about not living our lives unto Jesus Christ.

There is nothing sensible about not living our lives unto Jesus Christ.

There is nothing questionable about not living our lives unto Jesus Christ.

There is nothing debatable about not living our lives unto Jesus Christ.

There is nothing theoretical about not living our lives unto Jesus Christ.

There is nothing funny about not living our lives unto Jesus Christ.

There is nothing cheerful about not living our lives unto Jesus Christ.

There is nothing magnificent about not living our lives unto Jesus Christ.

There is nothing boastful about not living our lives unto Jesus Christ.

Our lives would be like an empty treasure chest if we don't live our lives unto Jesus Christ.

Our lives would be like a pregnant woman having a miscarriage if we don't live our lives unto Jesus Christ.

Our lives would be like a plane crash if we don't live our lives unto Jesus Christ.

Our lives would be like a famine if we don't live our lives unto Jesus Christ.

Our lives would be like a drought if we don't live our lives unto Jesus Christ.

There is nothing worthy about not living our lives unto Jesus Christ.

There is nothing beautiful about not living our lives unto Jesus Christ.

There is nothing loving about not living our lives unto Jesus Christ.

There is nothing intelligent about not living our lives unto Jesus Christ.

There is nothing genius about not living our lives unto Jesus Christ.
There is nothing lawful about not living our lives unto Jesus Christ.
Our life would be like being lost on a long voyage if we don't live our lives unto Jesus Christ.

The Earth's Ground

The earth's ground goes thousands of miles deeper than the ground that we live on every day.

The earth's ground holds all the ocean waters in place every day.

The earth runs deep beneath the ground that holds the mountains in place.

The earth runs deep beneath the ground that holds the hills in place.

The earth runs deep beneath the ground that holds the valleys in place.

The earth runs deep beneath the ground that holds the trees in place.

The earth runs deep beneath the ground that holds the volcanoes in place.

The earth runs deep beneath the ground that holds the islands in place.

The earth runs deep beneath the ground that holds the buildings in place.

The earth runs deep beneath the ground that holds you and me in place.

The earth runs deep beneath the ground that holds the roads in place.

The earth runs deep beneath the ground that holds he bridges in place.

The earth runs deep beneath the ground that holds the tunnels in place.

The earth runs deep beneath the ground that holds the forests in place.

The earth runs deep beneath the ground that holds the deserts in place.

The earth runs deep beneath the ground that holds houses in place.

The earth runs deep beneath the ground that holds water wells in place.

The earth runs deep beneath the ground that holds seashores in place.

The earth runs deep beneath the ground that holds beaches in place.

God created the heaven and earth and the earth runs very deep beneath the ground to give you and me a place to walk around on and run around on.

The earth runs deep beneath the ground to give you and me a place to spread the gospel of Jesus Christ wherever we go.

The earth runs deep beneath the ground that holds the seas, rivers, lakes, streams and ponds in place every day that you and I live on dry land above the rest of the ground that holds up the ocean waters every day.

God created the earth's ground to hold the deep ocean waters and the wet mulchy ground in place beneath the dry ground.

God created a lot more ground than water because beneath the oceans, rivers, seas, bays, lakes, ponds and streams it is the ground that holds them all in place all around the world.

God created the earth's ground for you and me to live on and love Him and keep His Commandments.

God didn't create us to live in the waters that run deep in the oceans.

God created the earth's ground to give you and me a place to live our lives unto Jesus Christ, who walked on the waters that the wet mulchy ground holds in place.

This comes to show that God created the earth's ground to be deeper than the oceans.

The ground gives us a place to stand as well as holding everything else in place around the world.

All Around the World

A man is a man all around the world.

A woman is a woman all around the world.

A boy is a boy all around the world.

A girl is a girl all around the world.

A teenager is a teenager all around the world.

Food is food all around the world.

Money is money all around the world.

Poverty is poverty all around the world.

Wealth is wealth all around the world.

Clothes are clothes all around the world.

Shoes are shoes all around the world.

Love is love all around the world.

Education is education all around the world.

Common sense is common sense all around the world.

The truth is the truth all around the world.

A lie is a lie all around the world.

A crime is a crime all around the world.

Motives are motives all around the world.

Intentions are intentions all around the world.

Marriage is marriage all around the world.

Divorce is divorce all around the world.

Intelligence is intelligence all around the world.

Genius is genius all around the world.

Excellence is excellence all around the world.

Health is health all around the world.

Sickness is sickness all around the world.

A hypocrite is a hypocrite all around the world.

A fool is a fool all around the world.

A friend is a friend all around the world.

Romance is romance all around the world.

A peace of mind is a peace of mind all around the world.

A hero is a hero all around the world.

Courage is courage all around the world.

A sinner is a sinner all around the world.

A murderer is a murderer all around the world.

A thief is a thief all around the world.

An adulterer is an adulterer all around the world.

An abuser is an abuser all around the world.

A fornicator is a fornicator all around the world.

A criminal is a criminal all around the world.

Life is life all around the world.

Grief is grief all around the world.

A smile is a smile all around the world.

A song is a song all around the world.

Medicine is medicine all around the world.

An illness is an illness all around the world.

Joy is joy all around the world.

Hope is hope all around the world.

Deceit is deceit all around the world.

Confusion is confusion all around the world.

Jealousy is jealousy all around the world.

Envy is envy all around the world.

Covetousness is covetousness all around the world.

A liar is a liar all around the world.

Death is death all around the world.

The grave is the grave all around the world.

An animal is an animal all around the world.

The heart is the heart all around the world.

A living soul is a living soul all around the world.

The head of the church is the head of the church all around the world, and the head of the church is Jesus Christ.

A Christian is a Christian all around the world.

Jesus Christ is Jesus Christ all around the world.

Every eye all around the world will see Jesus Christ on the clouds of glory.

Every saint all around the world will go with Jesus Christ back to heaven.

The redeemed are the redeemed all around the world.

The righteous are the righteous all around the world.

The holy are the holy all around the world.

The wicked are the wicked all around the world.

The children of God are the children of God all around the world.

A baby is a baby all around the world.

The wind is the wind all around the world.

A tree is a tree all around the world.

The grass is the grass all around the world.

Nature is nature all around the world.

A city is a city all around the world.

The country is the country all around the world.

The law is the law all around the world.

God's holy word is God's holy word all around the world.

The Holy Spirit is the holy spirit all around the world.

Sin is sin all around the world.

God's love is God's love all around the world.

God's grace is God's grace all around the world.

God's judgement is God's judgement all around the world.

God's justice is God's justice all around the world.

God's forgiveness is God's forgiveness all around the world.

God's mercy is God's mercy all around the world.

God's presence is God's presence all around the world.

God's victories are God's victories all around the world.

God's long suffering is God's long suffering all around the world.

God's salvation is God's salvation all around the world.

God's Son, Jesus Christ, is God's Son, Jesus Christ, all around the world.

The devil is the devil all around the world.

God is God all around the world.

Holding grudges is holding grudges all around the world.

Homosexuality is homosexuality all around the world.

Anger is anger all around the world.

Bad hygiene is bad hygiene all around the world.

Greatness is greatness all around the world.

The holy word is the holy word all around the world.

Prosperity is prosperity all around the world.

Feeblemindedness is feeblemindedness all around the world.

Overweight is overweight all around the world.

A bully is a bully all around the world.

Prison is prison all around the world.

A flower is a flower all around the world.

A boat is a boat all around the world.

A fisherman is a fisherman all around the world.

Politics are politics all around the world.

The military is the military all around the world.

Beautiful women are beautiful women all around the world.

The free will choice is the free will choice all around the world.

Work is work all around the world.

A workaholic is a workaholic all around the world.

Laziness is laziness all around the world.

An enemy is an enemy all around the world.

A broken heart is a broken heart all around the world.

Laughter is laughter all around the world.

Contentment is contentment all around the world.

Greed is greed all around the world.

Memory loss is memory loss all around the world.

Youth is youth all around the world.

Middle age is middle age all around the world.

Old age is old age all around the world.

Alzheimer's is Alzheimer's all around the world.

Cancer is cancer all around the world.

Cheer is cheer all around the world.

Believing in Jesus Christ is believing in Jesus Christ all around the world.

Loving Jesus and keeping His Commandments is loving Jesus and keeping His Commandments all around the world.

Mentally Advanced and Emotionally Retarded

There are many people who are mentally advanced in their education but emotionally retarded for feeling good about thinking they are never wrong about what they say and do.

There are many people who are mentally advanced in their intellect but emotionally retarded for feeling good about deceiving people.

There are many people who are mentally advanced in their genius but emotionally retarded for feeling good about manipulating people.

There are many people who are mentally advanced in their knowledge but emotionally retarded for feeling good about putting people down for their lack of knowledge.

There are many people who are mentally advanced in their wisdom but emotionally retarded for feeling good about making fun of people's ignorance.

Adam and Eve were mentally advanced in their knowledge of God, but they had become emotionally retarded for feeling good about eating that fruit from the tree of knowledge of good and evil.

Adam and Eve were mentally advanced in their talk with God, but they had become emotionally retarded when feeling good about living forever after disobeying God who told them not to eat from the tree of knowledge of good and evil.

Many people are mentally advanced in their knowledge of God's holy word but emotionally retarded for feeling good about wanting to be lord over God's flock existing from the book of Genesis to Revelation.

Christianity

Christianity has a big influence on this world every day.

Christianity is like the sun that shines all day long.

Christianity is like the full, white moonlight glowing all night long.

Christianity is like the sparkling stars shining all night long.

Christianity is like the great blue sky covering this world every day and night.

Christianity is like drinking clean fresh water.

Christianity is like eating healthy food.

Christianity is like getting a good night's sleep.

Christianity is like being in good health.

Christianity is like a warm gentle breeze.

Christianity is like a gold mine.

Christianity is like a high mountain.

Christianity is like a deep valley.

Christianity is like the ocean waves.

Christianity is like a beautiful house.

Christianity is like a bridge to cross over.

Christianity is like the river that flows into the ocean.

Christianity is like a mystery revealed.

Christianity is like a burning fire.

Christianity is like the dew that falls on the ground.

Christianity is like a beautiful red rose.

Christianity is like a bird that flies across the sky.

Christianity is like the wind that blows in different directions.

Christianity is like Jesus Christ who is the origin of Christianity for every true Christian to be like Jesus Christ all around the world.

Carry Me Through

My Lord Jesus, I need You to carry me through my disappointments because I have no strength to walk on my own through anything that disappoints me.

My Lord Jesus, I need You to carry me through my thoughts because I have no strength to walk on my own through anything that I think.

My Lord Jesus, I need You to carry me through my words that I say because I have no strength to walk on my own through whatever I say.

My Lord Jesus, I need You to carry me through my grief because I have no strength to walk on my own through my tears.

My Lord Jesus, I need You to carry me through my bad days because I have no strength to walk on my own through anything that goes wrong in the day.

My Lord Jesus, I need You to carry me through my heart because I have no strength to walk on my own through my motives and intentions that can catch me off guard and make me deceive myself into doing my own will instead of Your holy will, my Lord and Savior Jesus Christ.

My Lord Jesus, I need You to carry me though my free will choices because I have no strength to walk on my own through my free will choices that I can take for granted and make choices to live for this world that is no friend to You, my Lord Jesus, who doesn't need me who would deceive myself into believing that you need a sinner like me.

Many People Would Rather

Many people would rather hear words to please their flesh than hear words to please their spirit.

Many people would rather read books to please their flesh than read books to please their spirit.

Many people would rather eat foods that taste good but are bad for their health than eat food that doesn't taste good but is good for their health.

Many people would rather watch bad programs on TV to please their flesh than watch good programs on TV to please their spirit.

Many people would rather listen to songs to please their flesh than listen to songs to please their spirit.

Many people would rather do things to please their flesh than do things thing to please their spirit.

Many people would rather talk about things to please their flesh than talk about things to please their spirit.

There is nothing better to please the spirit than talking about the Lord.

There is nothing better to please the spirit than praying to the Lord.

There is nothing better to please the spirit than having faith in the Lord.

There is nothing better to please the spirit than trusting the Lord.

There is nothing better to please the spirit than waiting on the Lord.

There is nothing better to please the spirit than working for the Lord.

There is nothing better to please the spirit than living for the Lord.

If we live our life to please our flesh, we will sooner or later regret it.

If we live our life to please our flesh, it will shorten our life.

If we live our life to please our flesh, it will sooner or later leave us very empty on the inside.

If we live our lives to please our spirit, it will be pleasing to the Lord God Jesus Christ who is more willing to give us His Holy Spirit than a mother giving her new-born baby milk to drink.

Many people would rather turn their backs on the Lord to please their flesh than live for the Lord to please their spirit.

Many people would rather live in their sins to please their flesh than to live for the Lord God to please their spirit to worship God in spirit and truth.

The Lion's Den and Furnace Fire

We true children of God will be thrown into a spiritual lion's den and furnace fire for standing up for Jesus and not bowing down to the golden image of the world.

You and I will be thrown into the lion's den and furnace fire of criticizing words from non-Sabbath keepers who see us keeping the sabbath day holy on the seventh day of the week, which is Saturday and not Sunday.

You and I will be thrown into the lion's den and furnace fire of unbelievers' spiritualism because they believe that they can talk to the dead, but we show them the bible truth about the dead knowing nothing.

We true children of God will stand up for His Son, Jesus Christ, even though we will be thrown into the lion's den and furnace fire of unbelievers' false doctrines because we won't compromise the truth that will keep us rooted and grounded in God's holy word from the book of Genesis to the book of Revelation.

You and I can't be anything less than a true child of God for standing up for Jesus who shut the lions' mouths in the den and made it like a paradise to Daniel.

Jesus was also in the furnace fire and acted like a central cooling air conditioner to the three Hebrew boys.

Daniel and the three Hebrew boys didn't deny the true, living God, even when they faced death.

God didn't allow death to get victory over them.

You and I will be thrown into the lion's den and furnace fire of rejection by unbelievers for speaking the truth of God's holy word in love to them.

We all want to live to see Jesus come back again, but are we willing to be thrown into the lion's den and furnace fire of persecution for standing up for Jesus in this golden image of a sinful world.

If we miss out on heaven when Jesus comes back again, then it comes to show that we bowed down to worship the golden image of false pretense that is also in the church.

Daniel and the three Hebrew boys had nothing but true worship unto the true, living God, while the unbelievers in Babylon were full of false pretense worship which will one day become their lion's den and furnace fire of burning hell after the second resurrection.

The Highest Beauty

The highest beauty is not the lilies in the valley.

The highest beauty is not a shadow moving over the landscape.

The highest beauty is not a diamond ring.

The highest beauty is not a treasure chest.

The highest beauty is not jewelry.

The highest beauty is not the sunrise.

The highest beauty is not the sunset.

The highest beauty is not the full, white moonlight's glow.

The highest beauty is not the sparkling stars.

The highest beauty is not the glaciers on the mountain tops.

The highest beauty is not the puffy white clouds.

The highest beauty is not the great blue skies.

The highest beauty is not nature.

The highest beauty is not the oceans.

The highest beauty is not the tropical islands.

The highest beauty in this world is a beautiful woman on the inside and on the outside.

God created Eve to be the highest beauty in this world, where even the Garden of Eden wasn't more beautiful than Eve.

The serpent that tempted Eve was beautiful, but not more beautiful than Eve.

Adam couldn't resist Eve because she was so beautiful to him, and he ate the forbidden fruit she gave to him.

The highest beauty is a beautiful woman on the inside and on the outside that God had created from the beginning of time on earth.

There is nothing more beautiful than a beautiful Christian woman on the inside and on the outside, just like Queen Ester was in the bible.

The highest beauty is not a beautiful house.

The highest beauty is not a beautiful vehicle.

The highest beauty is not a beautiful building

The highest beauty is not a beautiful yard.

The highest beauty is not beautiful clothes.

The highest beauty is a beautiful woman on the inside and on the outside.

Even if she is poor, that can't take away her beauty that God gave to her.

Before I Was Born

God knew my thoughts before I was born.

God knew my words before I was born.

God knew my actions before I was born.

God knew my heart before I was born.

God knew my mind before I was born.

God knew my choices that I would make before I was born.

God knew my feelings before I was born.

God knew my fears before I was born.

God knew my failures before I was born.

God knew my disappointments before I was born.

God knew my sorrows before I was born.

God knew my joy before I was born.

God knew my accomplishments before I was born.

God knew my doubts before I was born.

God knew my dreams before I was born.

God knew my hardships before I was born.

God knew my life before I was born.

God knew my destiny before I was born.

God knew everything about me before I was born.

There is nothing that God didn't know about me before I was born.

God knew my purpose in life before I was born.

God knew all of my ups and downs in life before I was born.

God knew my name before I was born.

God knew my sins before I was born.

God knew my secrets before I was born.

God knew my mistakes before I was born.

God knew my flaws before I was born.

God knew my habits before I was born.

God knew my hereditary tendencies before I was born.

God knew my motives before I was born.

God knew my intentions before I was born.

God knew my past, present and future before I was born to know nothing.

Questions

Some questions that people ask are plain and simple.

Some questions that people ask are complicated.

Some questions that people ask are embarrassing.

Some questions that people ask don't make any good sense.

Some questions that people ask make good sense.

Some questions that people ask are ridiculous.

Some questions that people ask are demeaning.

Some questions that people ask are hurtful.

Some questions that people ask are deceitful.

Some questions that people ask are troublesome.

Some questions that people ask are disappointing.

Some questions that people ask are truthful.

Some questions that people ask are dishonest.

Some questions that people ask are bold.

Some questions that people ask are phony.

Some questions that people ask are convincing.

Some questions that people ask are good.

Some questions that people ask are bad.

Some questions that people ask are tricky.

Some questions that people ask are rewarding.

Some questions that people ask are deadly.

There were people who asked Jesus some questions that Jesus answered with the truth in love.

There were people who asked Jesus some questions that Jesus didn't answer.

There were people who asked Jesus some questions to trap Jesus into saying something wrong.

There were people who asked Jesus some questions that they knew were wrong to ask but they asked anyway because they were jealous of Jesus and the miracles he performed.

Questions are a wide-open door for anyone to walk through to especially always get their right answer from Jesus who can ask us a simple question that we can fail to answer truthfully.

Ashamed

There are people who feel ashamed about the hardships they have been through in their lives. For them, feeling ashamed makes them keep quiet about it and they don't use their hardships as a testimony about Jesus bringing them through their hard times.

This is wrong, because their hard times could be used to help others make it through their hardships.

No child of the Lord should feel ashamed about giving their testimonies about the hardships the Lord brought them through that can surely be used to encourage others who are going through their own hardships.

When church folks hold back their testimonies, the Lord holds back His blessings upon them.

Giving testimonies is a part of growing much stronger in the Lord so that we can make it through whatever is coming our way in the future that might not be good for us.

There is no shame in giving testimonies about the hardships that we didn't bring ourselves through.

There are some Christians who don't want to remember or say anything about the hardships they had in their lives.

They rob themselves of God's blessings for not giving any testimonies about what the Lord brought them through.

They feel ashamed and keep quiet about it because they don't want anyone to know that they had some hard times in their lives.

They want people to believe that they always had it good in their lives.

If Jesus felt ashamed about leaving heaven to live among sinners, then we all wouldn't be here today.

If Jesus felt ashamed of giving up His life on the cross to die to save us from our sins, then we all would be better off never being born.

This whole world would be better off to not exist if Jesus felt ashamed of coming to this world to redeem us back to God.

Will Not Reappear

Rebellion against God will not reappear among the angels in heaven because two-thirds of the angels in heaven did not rebel against God like the one third of the fallen angels did.

Pride will not reappear in heaven among the angels because it was those fallen angels who were proud of themselves and believed that they could rule over God.

They failed and were cast out of heaven forever and ever.

One day, God will destroy all the fallen angels in fire and brimstone, and He will also destroy all the wicked human beings who joined in with the fallen angels' rebellion against God.

Rebellion against God will not reappear in the new heaven and new earth that God will create for all of His obedient angels and all of his obedient children who will be made like the angels having no sins that will not reappear because of Jesus Christ who is cleansing the heavenly sanctuary with His blood that was shed on the cross to save us from our sins.

All of the angels in heaven are forever converted in Jesus Christ, who was Michael the Archangel being the commander who led the victory over all the fallen angels from heaven.

Rebellion against God will not reappear in heaven where all of God's righteous children will go when Jesus comes back again with all of His angels.

Rebellion and disobedience will never exist again after God creates a new heaven and new earth where no sin will exist among the angels and every human being who makes it to heaven.

There will be no reappearance of any kind of sin because no angel in heaven will make the mistake that Lucifer and the other fallen angels made when they rebelled against God in heaven.

No righteous child of God who enters into heaven will repeat any wickedness in heaven because Jesus Christ saved them from their sins that they confessed and repented of unto Jesus.

You and I must be saved in Jesus in this sinful world because God will not allow us to take or sins with us to heaven where Lucifer and his angels were cast out.

God is love, and sin is evil that God will not allow to reappear in the new heaven and new earth.

God will one day destroy the rebellion of sin forever and ever, making it impossible for sin to ever exist again.

No one will go to heaven with even one sin, no matter how many good and righteous deeds we do.

Jesus has paid it all to cleanse us and save us from our sins that cannot enter into heaven.

Many people live their lives rebelling against God, and will believe that they will enter into heaven along with their sins.

It doesn't work that way with God, who foreknew that His Son, Jesus Christ, was the only one who could save us from our sins.

Rebellion and disobedience will not reappear in the presence of God, because all the fallen angels and wicked human beings will one day be destroyed in fire and brimstone.

Sin will not reappear in the new heaven and new earth.

It will be like a bubble that bursts and can't reform its shape, so it will be gone forever from our eyesight.

No angel in heaven and no human being who makes it to heaven will have a thought, desire or inclination to want to rebel against God like Lucifer did.

It is like a mystery that Lucifer had everything except God's supreme authority on his holy throne.

For some reason, what God had given Lucifer wasn't enough for him.

He wanted to be God, and that caused him to sin against God who will not allow sin to reappear in heaven ever again.

God will not allow sin to exist forever so it spreads throughout the universe and other worlds because God is not an evil God.

Rebellion and disobedience against God is evil and it will not reappear in the new heaven and new earth that God will create after He destroys all the fallen angels and every wicked human being in fire and brimstone.

This will make it impossible for sin to reappear again in the new world.

There will be no other worlds of sin to exist because God has bound the fallen angels in the bottomless pit here on earth that God will make new one day with no reappearance of any kind or form of sin.

The only time that the rebellion of sin against God will reappear is in the second resurrection, where all the wicked dead will be raised up to join the fallen angels as they surround the new Jerusalem holy city to attack it.

This attack will fail because God will rain down fire and brimstone on them all and destroy them so they can never reappear with their sins.

If we confess and repent of our sins, Jesus will forgive us and cast our sins into the bottom of the sea to never reappear in our lives here on earth because we become a new creature in Him whose righteousness makes us right in God's holy eyesight.

When Jesus cleanses us of our sins, we are cleansed so that our sins won't reappear in our lives that we live unto Him who has no sins to appear before God to represent our case in heaven.

Jesus will not allow sins to reappear in heaven.

Lucifer and his fallen angels were cast out of heaven because of their sins of rebellion against God.

There will be no repeat of this because sin will never exist again to reappear in any angel in heaven or any human being who makes it to heaven for being saved in Jesus Christ who defeated the devil on the cross and when he rose from the grave to break the chains of sin from us.

No matter how much we claim to be a child of God in our daily living we must also appear that way before our neighbors and show them we are saved in Jesus.

If we hold onto even one sin, we will not enter into heaven with Jesus when He comes back again.

There will be no other devil and fallen angels and wicked human beings after they are destroyed in fire and brimstone by God, who will not fail to keep sin from reappearing in His holy and righteous presence.

When God eliminates sin, it will be gone forever and it will never reappear in the new heaven and new earth that God will create.

There will be no appearances of rebellion against God there.

If our sins reappear in our lives after we have been in communion with Jesus, then we never truly repented of our sins unto Jesus with a heart of deep remorse and desire to change from our sinful ways.

There will be no reappearance of any sins on our way back to heaven with Jesus who will take no one's sins with Him back to heaven.

Now is the time for us to confess and repent of all of our sins unto Jesus who will not reappear on the cross to save anyone from their sins.

What Jesus has done is for all existence that will not reappear with any sins ever again from anyone in heaven, where the free will originated to worship God and no other in His presence.

A movie will betray that the good guys destroyed the monsters, but the monsters will reappear and be worse than what they were before committing their evil destruction.

It will be no movie when God destroys the rebellion of wickedness that will not reappear and will never exist again after God destroys it all in fire and brimstone.

God will not allow sin to reappear in the new heaven and new earth where all the angels and all the saints will truly know what it means to love and obey our Creator.

What are You Going to do with Me?

Lord Jesus, what are You going to do with me who has a sinful nature to say something wrong?

Lord Jesus, what are You going to do with me who has a sinful nature to think wrong?

Lord Jesus, what are You going to do with me who has a sinful nature to do something wrong?

Lord Jesus, what are You going to do with me who has a sinful nature to be selfish?

Lord Jesus, what are You going to do with me who has a sinful nature to be proud?

Lord Jesus, what are You going to do with me who has a sinful nature to sin against You?

Lord Jesus, what are You going to do with me who can confess and repent of my sins because of Your goodness that leads me to repent?

Lord Jesus, what are You going to do with me who has a sinful nature to turn my back on You?

Lord Jesus, what are You going to do with me who has a sinful nature to do evil?

Lord Jesus, what are You going to do with me who is nothing without You?

Lord Jesus, what are You going to do with me who has a sinful nature to mess things up?

Lord Jesus, what are You going to do with me who You gave free will to love You or love the world?

Lord Jesus, what are You going to do with me who has a sinful nature to not know what to do with myself who You always know what to do with?

A Bad World

We are living in a bad world that will get much worse as time goes on.

This world is so uncertain every day that we don't know what bad things will happen next.

The bible says that in these last days there will be perilous times, and especially we Christians can see it so crystal clear.

This world became bad when Adam and Eve disobeyed God by eating that fruit from the tree of knowledge of good and evil.

Jesus came down from heaven to live among sinners in this bad world that Jesus overcame with His sinless life and death on the cross for all of our sins.

As time gets closer to the end of this bad world, more and more people will be lost in their sins for rejecting the Holy Spirit who teaches us all the truth about Jesus Christ who created this world perfect before Adam and Eve sinned against God.

We are living in a bad world where we need Jesus all the time to help us to live right unto Him because we can't live right unto Jesus with our own righteousness being like filthy rags every day in the presence of God.

Our righteousness can look so right to us in this bad world where the devil is full of evil and deception every day to cause us to eat the spiritual forbidden fruits of self-righteousness.

We are living in a bad world in these last days where the bad outweighs the good, but every child of God will go with Jesus to heaven when He comes back again, which this bad world can't stop from happening.

Learning is Eternal

Learning is eternal because we don't live long enough to learn about everything in this world.

There is so much to learn about the sea creatures.

There is so much to learn about the creatures down in the depths of the oceans.

There is so much to learn about all the animals.

Learning is eternal because there is always something new to learn about in this world.

There is so much to learn about human beings.

There is so much to learn about nature.

Learning is eternal because there is so much to learn about God's holy word.

There is so much to learn about the bible scriptures.

Learning is eternal because learning is non-stop, especially when it comes to learning more and more about Jesus Christ.

If we make it to heaven, we will forever be learning about the angels.

If we make it to heaven, we will forever be learning about creatures in other worlds.

If we make it to heaven, we will forever be learning about the universes.

If we make it to heaven, we will forever be learning about God the Father, the Son and the Holy Spirit.

Our life is short in this world where we don't live long enough to learn all the evils of sin that Jesus has exempted from eternity when He rose from the grave with the victory over death to be short beneath the heavens.

Learning is eternal because God is creating new eternal things beyond this world that will pass away even with so many things that we will never learn about, because we don't live long enough in this world to learn about everything in this world.

Are Like Trash

The technologies in this world are like trash compared to the technologies in heaven.

The technologies in this world are like trash compared to the technologies in other worlds.

The technologies in this world are like trash compared to the technologies that will be in the new Jerusalem holy city.

The technologies in this world are like trash compared to the technologies that will be in the new earth that God will create.

The technologies in this world are like trash compared to the technologies that Jesus is creating in our heavenly mansions.

The technologies in this world are temporary because they will one day pass away below Jesus' technologies that are eternal.

The greatest technologies in this world will be thrown in God's trashcan when Jesus comes back again to take us to heaven where Jesus' creations of technology will blow our minds in eternal amazement.

If Everything was Created by Chance

If everything was created by chance, then there would be no bible prophecy coming to pass.

If everything was created by chance, then there would be no truth in the bible, which says God created the heavens and earth.

If everything was created by chance, then all the chances that we take would be doomed to fail whether taking chances, good or bad, because chance has no mercy.

If everything was created by chance, then every theory would override the truth in our lives.

We would be like a fairy tale every day and the bible would have no truth about what we sow we shall reap.

If everything was created by chance, then all life forms would be like the air that has no substance to hold onto.

God is our substance in life that we can always hold onto, when chance is like the air that no one can hold onto.

If everything was created by chance, then the bible would be a lie for every Christian to throw away in the trashcan.

The source of all creations is God and not chance which is like a bad accident about to happen that we don't see coming our way and may not have the opportunity to escape.

If everything was created by chance, then we are all a train wreck piling up all existence with confusion, but no chance can override God's place on judgement day when He will judge everyone's false theories about chance creating all things.

Youth Comes Around Once in Life

Youth comes around once in life so youth is like pure gold.

Youth comes around once in life so youth is like a precious pearl.

Youth comes around once in life so youth is like a sparkling diamond.

Youth comes around once in life so youth is like a red ruby.

Youth comes around once in life so youth is like a beautiful love song.

Youth comes around once in life so youth is like the sun that shines.

Youth comes around once in life so youth is like the full moonlight's glow.

Youth comes around once in life so youth is like a bird flying so free across the sky.

Youth comes around once in life so youth is like the fresh air that we breathe in and out of our nostrils.

Youth comes around once in life so youth is like a beautiful red rose.

Youth comes around once in life so youth is like the shade under a tree on a hot summer day.

Youth comes around once in life so youth is like a high mountain.

Youth comes around once in life so youth is like a lily in the valley.

Youth comes around once in life so youth is like the stars that sparkle all night long.

Youth comes around once in life so youth is like a chest full of treasures.

Youth comes around once in life so youth is like riches and wealth.

Youth comes around in life in every generation, and then youth comes and goes into the guilty plea of old age.

When Jesus comes back again to take us to heaven, we will be young forever and ever in our immortal bodies.

We will never age and grow old in heaven because our youth will be eternal.

Youth comes around once in life, and so many of us took our youth for granted when we were young and foolish.

Youth comes around once in life but many young people today take their youth lightly and live a dangerous life.

Youth comes around once in life, so wise young people take it seriously so they don't make the same mistakes their parents and grandparents made.

Youth comes around once in life, so Jesus especially loves to use the youth to win souls to Him.

Youth comes around once in life so the youth have a true purpose to love Jesus and keep His Commandments.

Youth comes around once in life so the youth are so loved by Jesus who told His disciples that they must be humble like little children to enter into the kingdom of heaven.

I Can't Say that I have Arrived

When it comes to You, my Lord Jesus Christ, I can't say that I have arrived to be exactly like You twenty-four hours around the clock.

When it comes to You, my Lord Jesus Christ, I can't say that I have arrived to be exactly like You when I have sins to confess and repent of unto You.

When it comes to You, my Lord Jesus Christ, I can't say that I have arrived, when sanctification is a lifetime process.

When it comes to You, my Lord Jesus Christ, I can't say that I have arrived, when I will fall short of God's glory.

When it comes to You, my Lord Jesus Christ, I can't say that I have arrived, when on the spur of the moment I can say or do something wrong.

When it comes to You, my Lord Jesus Christ, I can't say that I have arrived, when Your Commandments will point out my sins to me.

Being saved in You, Lord Jesus Christ, is the only way that I can say I have arrived in the eyesight of God through Your Righteousness, my Lord Jesus Christ, even though my righteousness is like a filthy rag.

I can surely say that I have arrived when You, my Lord Jesus, come back again to take me to heaven where I will be exactly like You and have no sins.

Light Cannot Agree with Darkness

Light cannot agree with darkness twenty-four hours around the clock.

Good cannot agree with evil.

Wisdom cannot agree with foolishness.

Light and darkness cannot agree with anything.

The law cannot agree with crimes.

The truth cannot agree with lies.

Light cannot agree with darkness.

Peace cannot agree with war.

Love cannot agree with hate.

Wellness cannot agree with sickness.

Light cannot agree with darkness on any day.

Good hygiene cannot agree with body odor.

Kindness cannot agree with meanness.

Knowledge cannot agree with ignorance.

Light cannot agree with darkness, not even for one second.

A smile cannot agree with a frown.

A good name cannot agree with a bad reputation.

Working cannot agree with laziness.

Contentment cannot agree with greed.

Light cannot agree with darkness in the presence of God.

Right cannot agree with wrong.

Freedom cannot agree with slavery.

Equality cannot agree with discrimination.

Justice cannot agree with unfairness.

Light cannot agree with darkness, because God is light and the devil is darkness.

God cannot agree with the devil.

God cannot agree with sin and that is why God sent His only begotten Son to this dark world so He can save us from our sins.

God cannot agree with anyone who doesn't love Him and keep His Commandments.

God cannot agree with anyone who doesn't believe in His Son, Jesus Christ.

God cannot agree with those who are lost in their sins.

Light cannot agree with darkness because Jesus Christ is the light of the world to shine God's love all around the world, but darkness is of the devil who is like a roaring lion ready to devour you and me on any day.

Humility cannot agree with pride.

Courage cannot agree with fear.

Giving cannot agree with selfishness.

Faith cannot agree with living by eyesight.

Light cannot agree with darkness because God is light to reveal everything that we do, even in secret, and the devil is darkness who loves to spiritually blind anyone who walks in the darkness of sin.

The Church cannot agree with pretense.

God's holy word cannot agree with false doctrines.

A Christian cannot agree with a fool.

Light cannot agree with darkness because the light will shine through the dark.

Light cannot agree with darkness because the light will eliminate the dark.

Light cannot agree with darkness because God is everlasting light shining on this dark temporary world, and God will one day eliminate the darkness of sin in fire and brimstone.

The darkness of all wickedness will be destroyed beneath the eternal light of God who the devil is no match for.

The devil cannot overshadow even a dim light of God.

Over the Rainbow

Over the rainbow is the sun, moon and all the stars.

Over the rainbow are billions of galaxies.

Over the rainbow are endless black holes.

Over the rainbow are endless of other universes.

Over the rainbow are other worlds.

Over the rainbow are the heavens.

Over the rainbow are the holy angels.

Over the rainbow is Jesus Christ.

Over the rainbow is God.

Over the rainbow is eternal life.

Over the rainbow is everlasting love.

Over the rainbow is immortality.

Over the rainbow is perfect peace.

Over the rainbow is paradise.

Over the rainbow is no time.

Over the rainbow is no war.

Over the rainbow is no hate.

Over the rainbow is no jealously.

Over the rainbow is no disunity.

Over the rainbow is no favoritism.

Over the rainbow is no grudge.

Over the rainbow is no strife.

Over the rainbow is no heartache.

Over the rainbow is no grief.

Over the rainbow is no injustice.

Over the rainbow is no inequality.

Over the rainbow is no sickness.

Over the rainbow is no lie.

Over the rainbow is everlasting truth.

Over the rainbow is no pain.

Over the rainbow is no deformity.

Over the rainbow is no misfortune.

Over the rainbow is no age.

Over the rainbow is no retirement.

Over the rainbow is everlasting joy.

Over the rainbow is God sitting on His holy throne.

Over the rainbow is Jesus Christ on the right-hand side of God's holy throne.

Over the rainbow is Jesus in the heavenly sanctuary representing our case before God.

Over the rainbow is the book of life that is open with our names written in it, if we are saved in Jesus Christ.

Over the rainbow is heaven where we all want to go to with Jesus who created the rainbow as a sign for us to know that this world will not be destroyed by water again.

The rainbow is a sign of God's promise to us.

There is a perfect place over the rainbow where we want to go with all of our hopes and dreams that only Jesus can fulfill under the rainbow and over the rainbow.

Over the rainbow is no trouble.

Over the rainbow is no worry.

Over the rainbow is no fear.

Over the rainbow is no death.

Over the rainbow is no envy.

Over the rainbow is no sin.

Over the rainbow is heaven beyond this sinful world where a wish and luck are no foundation for anyone to stand on.

Over the rainbow is where Jesus is building us a heavenly mansion to live in forever and ever.

Over the rainbow is where all who are saved in Jesus will enter into heaven when Jesus comes back again.

Over the rainbow is where heaven is real beyond imaginary and made up wishes and dreams that can make us feel so good but have no real truth.

Only Jesus is forever and ever beyond the imaginary not existing over the rainbow where the unseen heaven is real.

Over the rainbow is no fairytale of make believe; that is only under the rainbow, which gives us false hopes and dreams.

Astronauts can fly into the outer space over the rainbow, but they can't enter into heaven with their sins that only Jesus can save them from so they can one day enter into heaven when He comes back again over the rainbow.

www.ingramcontent.com/pod-product-compliance
Lightning Source LLC
LaVergne TN
LVHW021237080526
838199LV00088B/4564